Addressing Special Educational Needs and Disability in the Curriculum: Science

The SEND Code of Practice (2015) reinforced the requirement that *all* teachers must meet the needs of *all* learners. This topical book provides practical, tried and tested strategies and resources that will support teachers in making science lessons accessible and exciting for all pupils, including those with special needs. The author draws on a wealth of experience to share her understanding of special educational needs and disabilities and show how science teachers can reduce or remove any barriers to learning.

Offering strategies that are specific to the context of science teaching, this book will enable teachers to:

- help all students develop their 'evidence-gathering' skills and aid their scientific discovery by involving the use of all the senses and structuring tasks appropriately;
- create a supportive environment that maximises learning opportunities;
- plan the classroom layout and display to enhance learning;
- use technology to adapt lessons to the needs of individual pupils;
- successfully train and fully use the support of their teaching assistants.

An invaluable tool for continuing professional development, this text will be essential for teachers (and their teaching assistants) seeking guidance specific to teaching science to all pupils, regardless of their individual needs. This book will also be of interest to SENCOs, senior management teams and ITT providers.

In addition to free online resources, a range of appendices provide science teachers with a variety of writing frames and activity sheets to support effective teaching. This is an essential tool for science teachers and teaching assistants, and will help to deliver successful, inclusive lessons for all pupils.

Marion Frankland has extensive experience of teaching science (as an Advanced Skills Teacher) in both mainstream and special schools. She is also a qualified SENCO.

Addressing Special Educational Needs and Disability in the Curriculum

Series Editor: Linda Evans

Children and young people with a diverse range of special educational needs and disabilities (SEND) are expected to access the full curriculum. Crucially, the current professional standards make it clear that *every* teacher must take responsibility for *all* pupils in their classes. Titles in this fully revised and updated series will be essential for teachers seeking subject-specific guidance on meeting their pupils' individual needs. In line with recent curriculum changes, the new SEND Code of Practice and other pedagogical developments, these titles provide clear, practical strategies and resources that have proved to be effective and successful in their particular subject area. Written by practitioners, they can be used by departmental teams and in 'whole-school' training sessions as professional development resources. With free web-based online resources also available to complement the books, these resources will be an asset to any teaching professional helping to develop policy and provision for learners with SEND.

The new national curriculum content will prove challenging for many learners, and teachers of children in Y5 and Y6 will also find the books a valuable resource.

Titles in this series include:

For a full list of titles see: www.routledge.com/series/SENCURR

Addressing Special Educational Needs and Disability in the Curriculum: Science

Second edition

Marion Frankland

Routledge
Taylor & Francis Group

LONDON AND NEW YORK

Second edition published 2017
by Routledge
2 Park Square, Milton Park, Abingdon, Oxon OX14 4RN

and by Routledge
711 Third Avenue, New York, NY 10017

Routledge is an imprint of the Taylor & Francis Group, an informa business

© 2017 Marion Frankland

First edition published by Routledge 2005

British Library Cataloguing-in-Publication Data
A catalogue record for this book is available from the British Library

Library of Congress Cataloging-in-Publication Data
A catalog record for this book has been requested

ISBN: 978-1-138-20904-6 (hbk)
ISBN: 978-1-138-20905-3 (pbk)
ISBN: 978-1-315-45785-7 (ebk)

Typeset in Helvetica
by Apex CoVantage, LLC

 Visit eResources: www.routledge.com/9781138209053

 Printed and bound in Great Britain by
TJ International Ltd, Padstow, Cornwall

Contents

Website materials

The following materials are available to download from our dedicated website and amend for your pupils as appropriate:

- CPD (continuing professional development) audit
- Model departmental policy (to amend)
- Entry activities: word search, labelling activity, anagrams
- Writing frame: presenting my results
- Homework activities
- DART activity (Cloze)
- Plenary game: dominoes
- A progress report letter for parents

Appendices

Series authors

The author

Marion Frankland (BSc, CSciTeach) has been teaching for 16 years and was an Advanced Skills Teacher of Science. She has extensive experience of teaching science at all levels in both mainstream and special schools and has worked as a SENCO in a special school, gaining her qualification alongside her teaching commitment.

A dedicated team of SEN specialists and subject specialists have contributed to this series.

Series editor

Linda Evans was commissioning editor for the original books in this series and has coordinated the updating process for these new editions. She has taught children of all ages over the years, and posts have included those of SENCO, Local Authority Adviser, Ofsted inspector and Higher Education tutor/lecturer. She was awarded a PhD in 2000 following research on improving educational outcomes for children (primary and secondary).

Since then, Linda has been commissioning editor for David Fulton Publishing (SEN) as well as editor of a number of educational journals and newsletters: she has also written books, practical classroom resources, Master's course materials and school improvement guidance. She maintains her contact with school practitioners through her work as a part-time ITT tutor and educational consultant.

SEND specialist

Sue Briggs has been supporting the education and inclusion of children with special educational needs and disabilities and their parents for over 20 years, variously as teacher, Ofsted inspector, specialist member of the SEN and

Disability Tribunal, school improvement partner, consultant and adviser. She holds a Master's degree in education, a first-class BEd and a diploma in special education (DPSE distinction). Sue was a national lead for the Achievement for All programme (2011–2013) and a Regional Adviser for the Early Support programme for the Council for Disabled Children (2014–2015) and is currently an independent education and leadership consultant.

Sue is the author of several specialist books and publications including *Meeting SEND in Primary Classrooms* and *Meeting SEND in Secondary Classrooms* (Routledge, July 2015).

Subject specialists

Art

Gill Curry was Head of Art in a secondary school in Wirral for 20 years and Advisory Teacher for Art and Gifted and Talented Strand Coordinator. She has an MA in Print from the University of Chester and an MA in Women's Studies from the University of Liverpool.

She is a practising artist specialising in print and exhibits nationally and internationally, running courses regularly in schools and print studios.

Kim Earle is Vice Principal at Birkenhead High School Academy for Girls on the Wirral. She has previously been a Head of Art and Head of Creative Arts, securing Artsmark Gold in all the establishments in which she has worked. Kim was also formerly Able Pupils and Arts Consultant in St Helens, working across special schools and mainstream schools with teaching and support staff on Art policy and practice. She still teaches Art in a mixed ability setting in her current school and works closely with local schools and outside organisations to address barriers to learning.

Design and technology

Louise T. Davies is founder of the Food Teachers Centre offering advice and guidance to the DfE and other organisations based on her years of experience as a teacher and teacher trainer and her role in curriculum development at QCA and the Royal College of Art. She led innovation at the Design & Technology Association, providing expertise for a range of curriculum and CPD programmes and specialist advice on teaching standards and best practice, including meeting special educational needs. Most recently, she has worked as Lead Consultant for the School Food Champions programme (2013–2016) and as an Adviser to the DfE on the new GCSE Food Preparation and Nutrition.

English

Tim Hurst began his career as an English teacher at the Willian School in Hertfordshire, becoming Second in English before deciding that his future lay in SEND. He studied for an Advanced Diploma in Special Educational Needs and has been a SEN coordinator in five schools in Hertfordshire, Essex and Suffolk. Tim has always been committed to the concept of inclusion and is particularly interested in reading development, which he passionately believes in as a whole-school responsibility.

Geography

Graeme Eyre has considerable experience of teaching and leading geography in secondary schools in a range of different contexts and is currently Assistant Principal for Intervention at an academy in inner London. Graeme is a consultant to the Geographical Association and a Fellow of the Royal Geographical Society. He has also delivered training and CPD for teachers at all levels. He holds a BA in Geography, a PGCE in Secondary Geography and an MA in Geography Education.

History

Ian Luff retired as Deputy Headteacher of Kesgrave High School in 2013 after a 32-year career during which he had been Head of History in four comprehensive schools and an Advisory Teacher with the London Borough of Barking and Dagenham. He is an Honorary Fellow of the Historical Association and currently works as an Associate Tutor on the PGCE history course at the University of East Anglia and as a Consultant in history education.

Richard Harris has been teaching since 1989. He has taught in three comprehensive schools, as history teacher, Head of Department and Head of Faculty. He has also worked as teacher consultant for secondary history in West Berkshire. Since 2001 he has been involved in history initial teacher education, first at the University of Southampton and more recently at the University of Reading. He has also worked extensively with the Historical Association and Council of Europe in the areas of history education and teacher training and has been made an Honorary Fellow of the Historical Association. He is currently Associate Professor in history education and Director of Teaching and Learning at the Institute of Education, University of Reading.

Languages

John Connor is a former head of faculty, local authority adviser and senior examiner. He has also served as an OFSTED team inspector for modern languages and special educational needs in mainstream settings. John was also an Assessor on the Advanced Skills Teacher programme for the DfE. He is currently working as a trainer, author and consultant and has directed teaching and learning quality audits across England, the Channel Islands, Europe, the Middle East and the Far East. He is also a governor of a local primary school.

Maths

Max Wallace has nine years' experience of teaching children with special educational needs. He currently works as an Advanced Skills Teacher at an inclusive mainstream secondary school. Appointed as a specialist Leader in Education for Mathematics, Max mentors and coaches teachers in a wide network of schools. He has previously worked as a Head of Year and was responsible for the continuing professional development of colleagues. He has a doctorate in Mathematics from Cardiff University.

Music

Victoria Jaquiss (FRSA) trained as a teacher of English and Drama and held posts of English teacher, Head of PSE, Music and Expressive Arts at Foxwood School. She became a recognised authority on behaviour management and inclusion with children in challenging circumstances. The second half of her career has involved working for the Leeds Music Service/ Leeds ArtForms as Steel Pan Development Officer and deputy inclusion manager/teacher. She was awarded the fellowship of the Royal Society of Arts in 2002.

Diane Paterson began teaching as a mainstream secondary music teacher. She went on to study how music technology could enable people with severe physical difficulties to make their own music, joining the Drake Music project in Yorkshire and becoming its regional leader. She then became inclusion manager/teacher at Leeds Music Service/ArtForms, working with children with additional needs. As secretary of YAMSEN: SpeciallyMusic, she now runs specialist regional workshops, music days and concerts for students with special/additional needs and those who care for them.

PE and sport

Crispin Andrews is a qualified teacher and sports coach and has worked extensively in Buckinghamshire schools coaching cricket and football and developing opportunities for girls in these two sports. He is currently a sports journalist, writing extensively for a wide range of educational journals, including *Special Children* and the *Times Educational Supplement*, and other publications such as *Cricket World*.

Religious education

Dilwyn Hunt taught RE for 18 years before becoming an adviser first in Birmingham and then in Dudley. He currently works as an independent RE adviser supporting local authorities, SACREs and schools. He is also in demand across the country as a speaker on all aspects of teaching RE, in both mainstream and special settings. He is the author of numerous popular classroom resources and books and currently serves as the executive assistant on the Association of RE Inspectors, Advisers and Consultants.

A few words from the series editor

The original version of this book formed part of the 'Meeting SEN in the Curriculum' series which was published ten years ago to much acclaim. The series won a BERA (British Educational Resources Award) and has been widely used by ITT providers, their students and trainees, curriculum and SEN advisers, department heads and teachers of all levels of experience. It has proven to be highly successful in helping to develop policy and provision for learners with Special Educational Needs or Disabilities.

The series was born out of an understanding that practitioners want information and guidance about improving teaching and learning that is *relevant to them* – rooted in their particular subject, and applicable to pupils they encounter. These books exactly fulfil that function.

Those original books have stood the test of time in many ways – their tried and tested, practical strategies are as relevant and effective as ever. Legislation and national guidance has moved on however, as have resources and technology; new terminology accompanies all of these changes. For example, we have changed the series title to incorporate the acronym 'SEND' (Special Educational Needs or Disability) which has been adopted in official documents and in many schools in response to recent legislation and the revised Code of Practice. The important point to make is that our authors have addressed the needs of pupils with a wide range of special or 'additional' needs; some will have Educational, Health and Care (EHC) plans which have replaced 'statements', but most will not. Some will have identified 'syndromes' or 'conditions' but many will simply be termed 'low attainers'; pupils who, for whatever reason, do not easily make progress.

This second edition encompasses recent developments in education, and specifically in Science teaching. At the time of publication, education is still very much in an era of change; our national curriculum, monitoring and assessment systems are all newly fashioned and many schools are still adjusting to changes and developing their own ways forward. The ideas and guidance contained in this book however, transcend the fluctuations of national politics and policy and provide a framework for ensuring that pupils with SEND can 'enjoy and achieve' in their Science lessons.

NB: The term 'parent' is used throughout and is intended to cover any adult who is a child's main care-giver.

Linda D. Evans

Acknowledgements

Our thanks to the staff and pupils of St John's CoE Middle School in Bromsgrove and Queensbury School in Erdington for allowing us to use their photographs.

Introduction

Ours to teach

Your class: 30 individuals to teach – to encourage, motivate and inspire: 30 individuals who must be seen to make good progress regardless of their various abilities, backgrounds, interests and personalities. This is what makes teaching so interesting!

Jason demonstrates very little interest in school. He rarely completes homework and frequently turns up without a pen. He finds it hard to listen when you're talking and is likely to start his own conversation with a classmate. His work is untidy and mostly incomplete. It's difficult to find evidence of his progress this year.

Zoe tries very hard in lessons but is slow to understand explanations and has difficulty in expressing herself. She has been assessed as having poor communication skills, but there is no additional resourcing for her.

Ethan is on the autistic spectrum and finds it difficult to relate to other people, to work in a group and to understand social norms. He has an Education, Health and Care plan which provides for some teaching assistant (TA) support, but this is not timetabled for all lessons.

Do you recognise these youngsters? Our school population is now more diverse than ever before, with pupils of very different abilities, aptitudes and interests, from a wide range of cultures, making up our mainstream and special school classes. Many of these learners will experience difficulties of some sort at school, especially when they are faced with higher academic expectations at the end of KS2 and into KS3–4.

Whether they have a specific special educational need like dyslexia, or are on the autistic spectrum or for various reasons cannot conform to our behavioural expectations – **they are ours to teach**. Our lessons must ensure that each and every pupil can develop their skills and knowledge and make good progress.

How can this book help?

The information, ideas and guidance in this book will enable teachers of Science (and their teaching assistants) to plan and deliver lessons that will meet the individual needs of learners who experience difficulties. It will be especially valuable to subject teachers because the ideas and guidance are provided within a subject context, ensuring relevance and practicability.

Teachers who cater well for pupils with Special Educational Needs and Disabilities (SEND) are likely to cater well for *all* pupils – demonstrating outstanding practice in their everyday teaching. These teachers have a keen awareness of the many factors affecting a pupil's ability to learn, not only characteristics of the individual but also aspects of the learning environment that can either help or hinder learning. This book will help practitioners to develop strategies that can be used selectively to enable each and every learner to make progress.

Professional development

Our education system is constantly changing. The national curriculum, SEND legislation, examination reform and significant change to Ofsted inspection means that teachers need to keep up to date and be able to develop the knowledge, skills and understanding necessary to meet the needs of all the learners they teach. High quality continuing professional development (CPD) has a big part to play in this.

Faculties and subject teams planning for outstanding teaching and learning should consider how they regularly review and improve their provision by:

- Auditing
  a) The skills and expertise of current staff (teachers and assistants)
  b) Their professional development needs for SEND, based on the current cohorts of pupils
  [There is an audit pro forma on the accompanying website]
- Using the information from the two audits to develop a CPD programme (using internal staff, colleagues from nearby schools and/or consultants to deliver bespoke training)
- Enabling teachers to observe each other, teach together and visit other classrooms and other schools

- Encouraging staff to reflect on their practice and feel comfortable in sharing both the positive and the negative experiences
- Establishing an ethos that values everyone's expertise (including pupils and parents who might be able to contribute to training sessions)
- Using online resources that are readily available to support workforce development (e.g., http://www.nasen.org.uk/onlinesendcpd/)
- Encouraging staff to access (and disseminate) further study and high quality professional development

This book, and the others in the series, will be invaluable in contributing to whole-school CPD on meeting special educational needs and in facilitating subject-specific staff development within departments.

1 Meeting special educational needs

Your responsibility

New legislation and national guidance in 2015 changed the landscape of educational provision for pupils with any sort of 'additional' or 'special' needs. The vast majority of learners, including those with 'moderate' or 'mild' learning difficulties, weak communication skills, dyslexia or social/behavioural needs, rarely attract additional resources: they are very much accepted as part of the 'mainstream mix'. Pupils with more significant special educational needs and/or disabilities (SEND) may have an Education, Health and Care plan (EHC plan): this outlines how particular needs will be met, often involving professionals from different disciplines and sometimes specifying adult support in the classroom. Both groups of pupils are ultimately the responsibility of the class teacher, whether in mainstream or special education.

> High quality teaching that is differentiated and personalised will meet the individual needs of the majority of children and young people. Some children and young people need educational provision that is additional to or different from this. This is special educational provision under Section 21 of the Children and Families Act 2014. Schools and colleges *must* use their best endeavours to ensure that such provision is made for those who need it. Special educational provision is underpinned by high quality teaching and is compromised by anything less.
>
> (SEND Code of Practice 2015)

There is more information about legislation (The Children and Families Act 2014; The Equality Act 2010) and guidance (SEND Code of Practice) in Appendix 1.1.

Definition of SEND

A pupil has special educational needs if he or she:

- Has a significantly greater difficulty in learning than the majority of others of the same age or
- Has a disability which prevents or hinders him or her from making use of facilities of a kind generally provided for others of the same age in mainstream schools or mainstream Post-16 institutions

(SEND Code of Practice 2015)

The SEND Code of Practice identifies four broad areas of SEND, but remember that this gives only an overview of the range of needs that should be planned for by schools; pupils' needs rarely fit neatly into one area of need.

Whole-school ethos

Successful schools are proactive in identifying and addressing pupils' special needs, focusing on adapting the educational context and environment rather than on 'fixing' an individual learner. Adapting systems and teaching programmes rather than trying to force the pupil to conform to rigid expectations will lead to a greater chance of success in terms of learning outcomes. Guidance on whole-school and departmental policy making can be found in Appendix 1.2, and a sample departmental policy for SEND can be downloaded from our website at www.routledge.com/9781138209053.

Table 1.1 The four broad areas of SEND

Communication and interaction	Cognition and learning	Social, emotional and mental health difficulties	Sensory and/or physical needs
Speech, language and communication needs (SLCN) Asperger syndrome and autism (ASD)	Specific learning difficulties (SpLD) Moderate learning difficulties (MLD) Severe learning difficulties (SLD) Profound and multiple learning difficulties (PMLD)	Mental health difficulties such as anxiety or depression, self-harming, substance abuse or eating disorders Attention deficit disorders, attention deficit hyperactivity disorder or attachment disorder	Vision impairment (VI) Hearing impairment (HI) Multi-sensory impairment (MSI) Physical disability (PD)

Policy into practice

In many cases, pupils' individual learning needs will be met through differentiation of tasks and materials in their lessons; sometimes this will be supplemented by targeted interventions such as literacy 'catch-up' programmes delivered outside the classroom. A smaller number of pupils may need access to more specialist equipment and approaches, perhaps based on advice and support from external specialists.

The main thrust of the Children and Families Act and chapter 6 of the SEND Code of Practice is that outcomes for pupils with SEND must be improved and that schools and individual teachers must have high aspirations and expectations for all.

In practice, this means that pupils should be enabled to:

- **Achieve their best**: additional provision made for pupils with SEND will enable them to make accelerated progress so that the gap in progress and attainment between them and other pupils is reduced. Being identified with SEND should no longer be a reason for a pupil making less than good progress.
- **Become confident individuals living fulfilling lives**: if you ask parents of children with SEND what is important to them for their child's future they often answer 'happiness, the opportunity to achieve his or her potential, friendships and a loving family' – just what we all want for our children. Outcomes in terms of well-being, social skills and growing independence are equally as important as academic outcomes for children and young people with SEND.
- **Make a successful transition into adulthood, whether into employment, further or higher education or training**: decisions made at transition from primary school in Year 7 and beyond should be made in the context of preparation for adulthood. For example, where a pupil has had full-time support from a teaching assistant in primary school, the secondary school's first reaction might be to continue this level of support after transition. This may result in long-term dependency on adults, however, or limited opportunities to develop social skills, both of which impact negatively on preparation for adulthood.

Excellent classroom provision

Later chapters provide lots of subject-specific ideas and guidance on strategies to support pupils with SEND. In Appendix 1.3 you will find useful checklists to help you support pupils with identified 'conditions', but there are some generic approaches that form the foundations of outstanding provision, such as:

- Providing support from adults or other pupils
- Adapting tasks or environments
- Using specialist aids and equipment as appropriate

The starting points listed in the following provide a sound basis for creating an inclusive learning environment that will benefit *all* pupils, while being especially important for those with SEND.

Develop pupils' understanding through the use of all available senses by:

- Using resources that pupils can access through sight *and* sound (and where appropriate also use the senses of touch, taste and smell to broaden understanding and ensure stronger memory)
- Regularly employing resources such as symbols, pictures and film to increase pupils' knowledge of the wider world and contextualise new information and skills
- Encouraging and enabling pupils to take part in activities such as play, drama, class visits and exploring the environment

Help pupils to learn effectively and prepare for further or higher education, work or training by:

- Setting realistic demands within high expectations
- Using positive strategies to manage behaviour
- Giving pupils opportunities and encouragement to develop the skills to work effectively in a group or with a partner
- Teaching all pupils to value and respect the contribution of others
- Encouraging independent working skills
- Teaching essential safety rules

Help pupils to develop communication skills, language and literacy by:

- Making sure all pupils can see your face when you are speaking
- Giving clear, step-by step instructions and limiting the amount of information given at one time
- Providing a list of key vocabulary for each lesson
- Choosing texts that pupils can read and understand
- Making texts available in different formats, including large text, symbols or screen reader programmes
- Putting headings and important points in bold or highlighting to make them easier to scan
- Presenting written information as concisely as possible, using bullet points, images or diagrams

Support pupils with disabilities by:

- Encouraging pupils to be as independent as possible
- Enabling them to work with other, non-disabled pupils
- Making sure the classroom environment is suitable, e.g., uncluttered space to facilitate movement around the classroom or lab; adapted resources labelled and accessible
- Being aware that some pupils will take longer to complete tasks, including homework
- Taking into account the higher levels of concentration and physical exertion required by some pupils (even in activities such as reading and writing) that will lead to increased fatigue for pupils who may already have reduced stamina
- Being aware of the extra effort required by some pupils to follow oral work, whether through use of residual hearing, lip reading or signed support, and of the tiredness and limited concentration which is likely to ensue
- Ensuring all pupils are included, and can participate safely, in school trips and off-site visits

These and other, more specific strategies are placed in the context of supporting particular individuals described in the case studies in Chapter 6, 'Real Pupils in Real Classrooms'.

2 An inclusive learning environment

Science is all about discovery. The greatest discoveries have been made when scientists observe particular phenomena, generate ideas to explain these and then search for further evidence to either prove or disprove these ideas. As part of this evidence-gathering process a scientist needs to employ a range of practical skills which include making observations that involve the use of all the senses. It is our job, as teachers, to develop all these skills in our pupils.

Pupils with special educational needs might find various parts of this discovery process more challenging than other pupils. This chapter considers how we can minimise any barriers that might make the subject inaccessible to pupils. The objective is to create a supportive environment which will maximise learning opportunities, make lessons more efficient and allow the pupils to focus on scientific learning.

The physical environment

Scientific laboratories are not always the most pupil-friendly environments, and, whilst the philosophy and practice of the teaching of science have changed over the last few years, many of the rooms in which it is taught have changed very little. Ask most parents what a school science laboratory is like and they will remember benches, high stools, even the smell of the laboratory. In many schools, very little has changed.

A great deal of time is spent in lesson preparation and marking pupils' work, but the actual layout of the room is often not given the priority it deserves. Even the colour of the walls can have an influence on the pupils. Most science teachers have little control over the positioning of things such as gas taps and the type of furniture in the laboratory, but, where opportunities arise, planning the layout of furniture and equipment carefully can have a great influence on the performance of pupils. The creation of discrete features such as quiet areas can only enhance scientific learning. Never be afraid to change things around, and if it does not work, change it again. Difficulties can arise when teachers do not have the luxury of their own laboratory but rather have to share; discussion between colleagues is essential, especially when trying to improve the learning environment for pupils with SEND.

Considerations

- The furniture and how it is arranged to allow access to all areas and services and to allow the pupils to work in appropriate pairs and groups
- The use of colour and wall displays
- Equipment and its placement and labelling

Furniture should be arranged, wherever possible, to allow access for all pupils, including those in wheelchairs or with walking aids. (Pupils with visual impairment [VI] will benefit from the room layout remaining constant but will cope with furniture being moved around if this is pointed out to them.)

Benches may be static, but seating can usually be moved around to allow for pupils being able to see the board, a demonstration or an interactive whiteboard. Is the room flexible enough to allow pupils the opportunity of grouping together for any discussion work? All these are important points.

Consider the amount of furniture in the room. Is there too much? Tidy storage of coats and bags is an important point of safety in all situations, but for pupils with visual impairment and mobility difficulties it is even more so.

Do any of the pupils require benches that are height adjusting to accommodate wheelchairs? This furniture may not be permanently required, but discussion is needed with the special needs department within the school to see what provision can be made for the duration of the time certain pupils spend in the laboratory. There are a number of specialist suppliers of such furniture, and they can supply adjustable desks to cater for the different heights of wheelchairs and adjustable-height chairs for pupils with posture difficulties. If pupils feel comfortable in the laboratory, they are more likely to engage in the lesson.

Specialist equipment for pupils with VI can often be borrowed from the LA Sensory Support Service. Sloping desktops, magnifiers and specially adapted science equipment such as scales and thermometers with large-format gradations are often useful for other pupils too.

Walls and displays

If we are to avoid sensory overload (which can be an issue for pupils on the ASD spectrum especially), but want to create the best learning environment for our pupils, the colours used in the laboratory are important. The colour of the walls is often out of the hands of the teacher, but improvements can be achieved with backing paper, posters and pupils' work. Colours do seem to affect people: most pastel colours are calming, especially pale greens; dark blue is depressing; red provokes anger and yellow is seen as uplifting.

It is important to plan how to organise wall coverings and have some areas that are changed frequently, especially if things such as key words and objectives are displayed. Wall covering may include:

- Pupils' work
- Objectives
- Key words (and meanings)
- Posters related to units being covered
- Science posters, e.g., on safety
- Spelling of common scientific words
- Pieces of equipment to illustrate work or stimulate interest

Care is needed not to make walls so busy that they become a distraction for pupils. Give careful consideration to the placement of displays and label clearly so that they can be seen from a distance and have meaning for the pupils. Place at a suitable height – if the teacher is over six feet tall, he will have a very different view of things to a Year 7 pupil who is four feet six inches tall or a Year 9 pupil seated in a wheelchair.

It is important to select a range of pupil work to display on the walls to celebrate their successes and achievements. It would be all too easy just to display the neatest and most colourful work, which is often just representative of a few of the pupils in the class. This can also favour girls; why not have a count of the number of boys and number of girls represented in the displays in your lab and see if there is a balance? Every pupil needs to have their successes celebrated. Displayed work can be much more meaningful with a comment from the teacher to say why that particular piece has won a place in the display. Displaying photographs of pupils engaged in practical work can overcome the situation where some pupils never produce the sort of work which looks good on the wall.

It is important to share the objectives and outcomes of the lesson with the pupils, and this is discussed further in Chapter 5. It is good practice to display these objectives and outcomes throughout the lesson so the pupils can refer to them to help target their work.

Key word lists can be valuable for helping pupils use the correct scientific terminology and the correct spellings. Static displays of key words soon become 'wallpaper', however, which pupils no longer notice. These words need to be changed regularly and explained as they go up on the wall. The words become more meaningful if they are supported with definitions and if they are used in the lessons. These can be made into games, quizzes and quick revision.

Owing to the number of groups a science teacher may have in the classroom each day, consideration needs to be paid to where these are displayed, and they need to be large enough for pupils to see. It may also be important to colour-code them for each group or year. It may be useful to use pictures, diagrams or symbols with key words; this is especially helpful to pupils with learning difficulties.

Certain colour combinations of words and backgrounds can be difficult to read for some pupils. As a general rule of thumb, if the words are to be read close up, then a dark colour on a pale background is best; however, if the displays are to be read from a distance, then pale colours (such as yellow or white) on dark backgrounds (such as dark blue) are often easier to read. You do, however, need to consider pupils with colour blindness, and some colour combinations can be easier for pupils with dyslexia; the best solution is to ask the pupils which colour combinations they find easiest to read. This could even be the subject of an investigation.

Equipment within the laboratory

Apparatus needs to be clearly labelled and placed in accessible areas. It may be appropriate and time saving to prepare apparatus before the start of a practical lesson. This will help those pupils who have poor organisational skills and allow them to actually get on with the investigation. It is good practice to group apparatus together, for example have heating apparatus, such as Bunsen burners, bench mats, tripods and gauzes, within the same area; this cuts down unnecessary movement.

For those pupils who experience motor skills difficulties, consider having adapted apparatus available. There are a number of suppliers of adapted apparatus, such as NRS Healthcare (see Resources for contact details). Alternatively, you can consider adapting standard apparatus to meet the needs of your pupils. For example, many pupils with poor motor skills find it difficult to use a Bunsen burner. You can solder a piece of metal, to act as a lever, which enables these pupils to move the collar around without having to use the thumb and first finger. The type of flame can now be altered with just a knuckle. (Make sure that equipment is well-maintained to ensure smooth working.)

When adapting apparatus, it is essential to think about safety. Check with CLEAPPS and the health and safety officer in your school to ensure the apparatus would be considered safe. Adapted apparatus could include:

- Gauze laced to the top of the tripod to stop it being accidentally knocked off
- Plastic measuring jugs instead of measuring cylinders if approximate amounts are required
- A small funnel when there is no option but to use a measuring cylinder
- Foam collars around the measuring cylinder to enable a better grip
- For sensory-impaired pupils, a moisture sensor connected to a buzzer to buzz (or a light to light) when a container is full
- Rims of glassware painted in black to make it easier for some visually impaired pupils to see
- A foam collar around a thermometer to allow easier grip
- Pieces of non-slip material on which to stand apparatus
- Very shallow trays that pupils can put apparatus in so that if substances are spilt they are contained
- Protective aprons/lab coats
- Book rests
- A free-standing magnifying glass
- Pupils with visual impairments might find reading scales difficult, particularly on things such as thermometers that have small scales; for these pupils you can use talking thermometers and instruments with tactile scales

This equipment could be stored with the other items or put into trays forming sets of apparatus. It is good practice to have a few sets available; this enables all those pupils who feel in need of extra support to appreciate the value of the apparatus, and it does not make pupils with a particular difficulty feel different from the rest of a group and so aids their self-esteem. When demonstrating experiments, use the adapted apparatus sometimes.

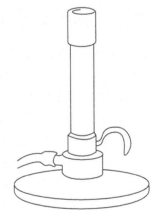

Other adaptations that may be useful include:

- Using retort stands for beakers and test tubes so that pupils can support apparatus; this is useful for pupils with limited motor skills; if the jaws of the clamp are not closed fully, they can slide the apparatus in or out easily
- Putting foam around the handles of test tube holders and crucible tongs to increase the grip for those with poor motor skills
- Putting a little Vaseline onto beakers to see when they are warm, as pupils will be able to see it melt (chocolate can also be used but can be a little messy)
- For stirring, use a magnetic stirrer; these can reduce spills, which is particularly important when using harmful chemicals

Practical work can be rewarding for pupils with sensory or motor difficulties if the equipment is carefully considered and adaptations made when necessary. The important thing is to consider the problems the pupils are having and come up with a piece of apparatus to suit their requirements, allowing them access to the curriculum and increasing their self-esteem. If there is a teaching assistant who knows the pupils well, use their invaluable insights into the needs of individuals, and ask their advice about pre-empting problems.

(Teachers may have problems appreciating the difficulties experienced by some pupils. Appendix 2.1 contains some ideas that could be used during a faculty meeting for SEND training. Tasks such as fastening buttons whilst wearing thick gardening gloves, with someone asking you questions at the same time, demonstrate how the physical act detracts from the content of the work.)

Clear labelling of apparatus and substances is essential. It is possible to buy labelling machines that type in Braille; the dual labelling of trays can be useful for those pupils with visual difficulties. Colours and symbols will help some pupils, so try using a system of colour-coding and diagrams when labelling apparatus. It is worth making a room plan of where key apparatus is stored and displaying this on the wall to help those pupils likely to forget. You could also give a plan to anyone assisting in the laboratory.

The communicating classroom

Communication can take many forms, with written and spoken language being the most obviously recognisable ones. However, the way we speak, our body language or even what is not said can be equally important. There are many skills involved in being an effective communicator. As teachers we need to develop and practise these skills but also teach them to pupils. Other adults who interact with pupils, such as teaching assistants and laboratory technicians, also need to be aware of the importance of good communication and act as good role models.

It is vital that teachers speak clearly and unambiguously to pupils, using scientific terminology relevant to the age and ability of the various pupils in the group. This may sound like common sense, but language and tone have an important role to play in allowing pupils to access the curriculum. Be prepared to repeat key concepts or instructions, and, if pupils ask what seem to be obvious questions, try to answer with patience, keeping the tone of your voice even rather than giving the impression that you are frustrated at having to repeat things for them. It may also be important to have a copy of key points, objectives and instructions on the board or available for individual pupil use.

Clear explanations of terminology can prevent a lot of misunderstanding and failure (some possibilities for confusion are listed in the following). Remember that for pupils with learning difficulties, especially those with hearing impairments and those on the autistic spectrum, the use of metaphor can be misleading (an explosion of colour, killer explosion).

> ## Words with more than one meaning
> - Solution
> - Resistance
> - Concentration
> - Light
> - Rays/raise

Questioning skills

Questioning is a key skill for any teacher. We do not just ask questions to test if the pupils understand a certain concept; we want to help them develop their ideas. Verbalising an idea helps it become more secure. This is therefore even more important for some pupils with special educational needs. Verbal reasoning provides a vehicle for these pupils to express their ideas without the burden of having to write. When written accounts are required, skilful questioning can prepare pupils for the writing task and help them organise their thoughts.

Questions can vary greatly in their level of conceptual difficulty, and there are different ways of categorising these: perhaps the most used of these is called Bloom's Taxonomy (Bloom 1976). Bloom's Taxonomy and how it can be related to questions is shown in Table 2.1.

Table 2.1 Bloom's taxonomy

Classification	Definition	Active words
Knowledge	Knowing facts and describing what is observed	Define, state, list, name, write, recall, recognise, identify
Comprehension	Using ideas in familiar contexts, explaining how and why something happens	Summarise, explain, interpret, classify, convert, illustrate, translate
Application	Using ideas, knowledge, understanding in a new context	Use, solve, apply, modify, relate, predict
Analysis	Breaking information down, seeking patterns	Deduce, contrast, distinguish, arrange, deconstruct, discuss, devise, plan, criticise, separate, break down
Synthesis	Generalising from given information, linking ideas and theories to make explanations or predictions	Restate, organise, generalise, derive, discuss, formulate
Evaluation	Comparing and discriminating between ideas, making choices based on reasoned argument, verifying the value of evidence	Summarise, judge, appraise, defend, argue, validate, compare, contrast, assess, verify

The first category, 'knowledge', is what is often described as 'closed' questioning: this is where there is normally only one answer which is correct. This type of question does not challenge the pupils to think and expand their ideas. It can also be disheartening to some pupils, who find it difficult to recall facts and ideas, to always get the answer to this type of question wrong.

As you progress through Bloom's Taxonomy, the conceptual demand, and therefore the level of challenge of the question, increases. Questions need to be directed towards individual pupils so that they are at the appropriate level to provide just enough challenge to extend the pupil. It is therefore important to prepare the key questions, around which the lesson is based, before the lesson starts.

'Big Questions' are those for which you would not expect there to be an immediate response: the pupils need to think about them and develop their ideas. It is often more appropriate for pupils to work in groups to share and develop their ideas for these Big Questions. The level of demand of the question can be changed by changing the way the question is phrased.

For example, the initial question might be: 'Name the seven life processes' – this question would be categorised as a 'knowledge' question, and the pupils would be able to get the answer completely right, partially right or wrong. This could be changed into a series of questions that ask the pupils to apply their ideas in science to different situations, for example: 'If all living things go to the toilet (excrete), how does a tree do this?' – this question would be categorised as a 'synthesis' question. It has a higher conceptual demand and is designed to get the pupils to think. Pupils may experience more success with this type of question because they are not simply being asked to recall; the ideas behind excretion are also more likely to become embedded as a result.

When asking any question you need to consider 'wait time': this is the time between when you finish asking the question and when you jump in because no one has answered it. Research suggests that the average wait time can be less than one second; this is too short a time for any pupil and especially so for many with SEND. It is therefore important to provide sufficient wait time. The length of wait time also depends on the type of question. A simple 'knowledge' question might need a wait time of a few seconds. However, a synthesis question, especially if it is being discussed in groups, might need several minutes.

To help the pupils understand what is expected of them, it is useful to signal the amount of time they have to answer the question. You could always start with, 'This is a four-second question . . .' It is also possible to buy large hourglass-style egg timers, which can range from about 30 seconds to about 15 minutes in time capacity. So, when you ask your Big Question, why not let the pupils know that it is a five-minute question to be discussed in groups and turn the hourglass over to let them know their time has started. There are also timers available online, which can be used on an interactive whiteboard.

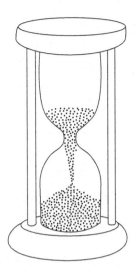

When asking questions of the whole class, if you allow the pupils to put their hands up to signal that they wish to answer the question, this will always encourage the same pupils to attempt to answer. Often, it is the pupils with special educational needs who miss out. The alternative is to develop a culture where the pupils do not expect to put their hands up; questions are therefore directed at individuals. This encourages all pupils to get involved. There is often an expectation that if the pupil is asked a question then he or she should attempt to answer it. This has an implication on the type of question you might ask of individual pupils. It might be inappropriate to ask a certain pupil to name the male parts of a plant because you know he or she has difficulty with recall-type questions. However, the same pupil might be asked to describe how he or she thinks a bee might collect pollen from a plant, and through the answer to this question you might encourage the pupil to use the names for the parts accurately.

Allowing pupils to ask questions is also a valuable form of communication. To develop confidence, allowing pupils to write down their question and read it out is useful. Having a question box and allowing pupils to write their own questions to put in can be a valuable activity and can be used as a valuable plenary session.

Working in groups

Speaking within a whole-group setting can be daunting for many pupils, and therefore working with a partner or within a small group can be valuable in developing their self-confidence. Similarly, reading aloud is very difficult for some pupils, and the chance to rehearse beforehand will result in a more successful outcome.

Within the laboratory paired group work is often used for practical sessions. At such times it is vital to ensure both pupils contribute to the actual work, even if the less confident one allows his or her partner or support assistant to take the lead role. However, as the class teacher it is important that you do not allow one of the pupils to 'hide behind' the other. It is easy to assume that pupils and support staff automatically know how to 'support' without taking over, but this is often not the case. A role-play activity demonstrating how to, and how not to, support learners and learning can be useful and make a significant and immediate impact.

Breaking the work down into smaller steps is important, especially in a practical session. Within the group there may be pupils with short attention spans, and unless the task is presented in smaller steps they may fail to complete the work successfully. This is also important for those pupils with literacy problems: if they are faced with a whole lesson of written work, they will find concentration a problem and may not complete the work or may become disruptive. Minimising the amount of writing required (and drawing of apparatus) allows more time to concentrate on doing and thinking about the science behind the practical work. There is rarely a need for pupils to produce a formal 'write-up' of the experiment, as it is the findings which are important. Ready-prepared record sheets can do a lot to speed up the process of recording and make it more accurate (see Appendices 2.2–2.4).

Speaking frames can be a valuable tool for developing scientific concepts and language. They can be used to establish a 'listen – imitate – innovate' model and instil confidence in pupils whose thinking/speaking skills are weak. Pupils can work in pairs, and mixing pupils of different abilities is often the most successful approach (see Appendix 2.5).

Setting the scene is important – outlining not only the task, but also the key features you will be looking for:

During preparation:

- Collaboration
- Reflecting on content and refining ideas
- Note-taking
- Rehearsal

Content of the work:

- Choice of topic
- Research skills
- Effectiveness
- Use of key words

During presentation:

- Use of speaking frame to speak in sentences and add sentences of their own
- Addition of relevant detail
- Good use of standard English as they speak
- Collaboration
- Pace of presentation
- Type of voice used

- Listeners engaged
- Good body language
- Dealing with problems

Appendix 2.5 shows how a speaking frame could be used for a key stage 3 topic about evaporation with a planning sheet and pupil presentation sheet. The same frame could be used for key stage 4 pupils, for example looking at the reactivity of groups within the periodic table.

Another useful tool is peer tutoring. This can take many forms but is basically an approach whereby pupils help each other. Peer tutoring works best when pupils have received some guidance in how to approach it – from both sides of the arrangement. (See rules of peer tutoring that follow.) It can also take the form of a pupil or group of pupils reporting back on the findings from their experiment to another small group. It is possible to use the same style of speaking frame as the prior but give each group a different topic. In this way, pupils can explain some of the key words to their peers. This might even result in a group of pupils presenting part of the lesson, maybe explaining how to perform an investigation or presenting it to the rest of the group. The important factor in peer tutoring is it gives pupils the opportunity to demonstrate their current knowledge, to extend their learning and to gain confidence. The extent of the peer tutoring needs to be directed by the classroom teacher, ensuring it is not always the same people who are chosen or volunteer for the role.

Rules of peer tutoring

If you are the tutor:

- Be clear about what you are trying to do.
- Help your partner do the work for themselves – don't do it for them.
- Ask if there is anything they don't understand.
- Be patient – don't rush.
- Be positive and encouraging.

If you are the tutee:

- Be clear about what you need to know or what you need to do.
- Ask questions that will help you understand – ask as many times as you need.
- Help your partner to help you – explain how you learn best.
- Have a go at the work yourself – don't expect your partner to do it for you.
- Be polite.

Numeracy and technology in the inclusive laboratory

For some pupils, the mathematical aspects of science are difficult. It is useful to develop posters of key mathematical concepts within the topic being covered. Some props, such as a number line, could be kept on the wall permanently for pupils to refer to when necessary. However, some pupils may prefer to be more discrete and use, for example, a ruler to help them with adding.

It is also important for the science and mathematics faculties to find time for some training as science teachers can confuse pupils by showing them alternative methods for mathematical calculations rather than using the techniques now taught in maths. This saves a lot of time and confusion. If joint departmental meetings are not possible, find out how, and when, staff in the mathematics faculty teach pupils to draw graphs and the language they use when encouraging pupils to subtract. For instance, do they use the term 'take away'? Do they use the number line? It is also valuable to check that pupils understand the systems of weights and measures used in science and how to add/subtract different amounts. Time can also be an issue for many pupils with special needs. Visual prompts for these aspects of work in science can be very valuable – either up on the wall or clipped into books/folders or as plastic-covered 'crib-sheets' on the benches. (See Appendices 2.6–2.14 for examples.)

New technologies

Technology is vital for an inclusive laboratory. It can enhance the work of both the pupil and the teacher. Pupils can report back via a PowerPoint presentation, or similar, or use an appropriately adapted worksheet. Depending on school policy, pupils could also use their own mobile phones or tablets to create Word documents or similar. This enables those pupils with a range of special needs to participate to a fuller extent as the written word can be redrafted, spell-checked and presented in an easily readable way.

Technology also provides a valuable tool for teachers, allowing us to adapt resources to suit the needs of individual pupils in a number of ways. You can alter the size of print, simplify language, make work more accessible through the use of DART (Directed Activity Related to Text; see Chapter 3) or draw tables for pupils to complete with data from observations. These should, of course, be saved in the shared area or uploaded to a Virtual Learning Environment (VLE) in order to share good practice with other teachers. It might be that pupils with SEND are given additional intervention sessions as part of their timetables; revisiting and revising work previously done in class (e.g., by accessing work through the VLE) can also be valuable.

By using tablets or digital cameras, experiments can be recorded so pupils have the opportunity to watch them again during the lesson if they do not fully understand a practical procedure. For some pupils, viewing a video clip of, for example, using a measuring cylinder correctly can be very useful. Lots of these videos exist on sites like YouTube or Vimeo.

Instructions for performing investigations and experiments are often an issue in science lessons. If you just give verbal instruction, there will always be a group of pupils who have not managed to follow all the steps. If you give written instructions, the readability of technical directions might cause problems for some pupils. If you do both, you could still run the risk of not reaching all pupils. One possible answer to this is to take photographs of someone performing the experiment and then present these as a sequence of steps within, for example, a PowerPoint presentation. By all means add instructions, and, when these refer to a piece of apparatus, you can draw an arrow onto the relevant item to illustrate this. It is possible for this type of presentation to keep restarting on a cycle and move on automatically, which would allow the pupils to work at their own pace and look up to find the correct stage.

Science is an ideal subject for the development of motor skills, but if the practical work is not essential for the learning objectives, then allowing pupils to use computer simulations enables them to access the scientific concepts. Computer simulations can also be used to reinforce concepts. For example, when studying radioactivity at key stage 4, the absorption of the different types of radiation can be demonstrated, and the pupils can then perform their own virtual experiments using a simulation such as RadiationLab (http://radiation-lab.software.informer.com). There are many apps and websites which allow pupils who struggle to manipulate equipment to carry out experiments alongside their peers.

With datalogging equipment, pupils do not have to record individual readings for an experiment and then plot a graph from each of these points. The computer software does this for them, and they can concentrate on developing scientific explanations for the shape of the graph. For pupils with motor skill problems, this enhances their progress as they have to spend little time on manipulating apparatus or graph paper. Pupils do need practice in drawing graphs, but it is important to consider the purpose of the graph in the context of the work.

By combining datalogging equipment with an interactive whiteboard, it is possible to demonstrate learning points without the pupils performing practical work.

This would not necessarily be the preferred teaching method every lesson, but there might be occasions where it is appropriate. For example, you might want to set up a cooling curve experiment using octadecanoic acid. This could run whilst the pupils are engaged in a different learning activity. The teacher could use the projected results from this to discuss melting points.

It is possible to use digital microscopes, which can be really useful for pupils who through either visual impairment or poor motor skills find it difficult to use a conventional microscope. By projecting the image onto the board, all pupils can be shown exactly what it is they are looking at or for.

For some pupils the use of Clicker software is a valuable tool. This can either be on a laptop or a tablet. By entering words for a particular topic (this could be done by the teaching assistant), the pupils will be able to concentrate on the scientific concepts rather than the words. Clicker can be used to support pupils' writing at several levels, enabling them to produce a smart-looking piece of work with correct spellings and in which they have been able to focus on recording what they know and understand or what they have observed rather than fret about the process of writing. Clicker is published by Crick Software (www.cricksoft.com) (Figure 2.1).

For pupils who need symbols to support their reading, Symwriter 2 can be purchased to use on laptops. This allows pupils to type, showing symbols related to the word as they go and allowing them to check that they have spelled words correctly. Alternatively, information can be input prior to the lesson which the pupils can then use to support their learning, either a list of

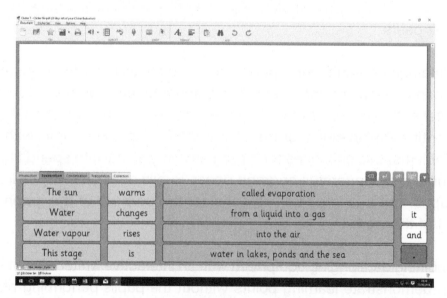

Figure 2.1 This is an example of a Clicker Grid which supports pupils in their recording and can be used as a means of checking their understanding. The grids can be designed by the teacher and therefore tailored to suit pupils' needs.

Source: Clicker 7 screenshots reproduced with permission from Crick Software – www.crick soft.com.

instructions to follow to carry out an experiment or some questions to prompt a discussion on what has been learned in that lesson.

There is a range of modified equipment available for pupils with special educational needs, including large-key keyboards, touchscreens and switch access devices, as well as an ever-growing range of apps for tablet computers. For further information and catalogues, see the References and the Resources and Useful Websites sections. Organisations such as the Association for Science Engineering (ASE; http://ase.org.uk) and Aiding Communication in Education (ACE; www.ace-centre.org.uk) are also on hand to offer advice and guidance.

Conclusion

Developing an inclusive laboratory is not without hard work. It is important to have a good knowledge of the strengths and weaknesses of the pupils, use the support that may be provided wisely and build on your own skills. If one thing fails, do not give up, but evaluate where things went wrong in order to develop the approach for the next time.

It is important to consider the following when developing an inclusive laboratory:

- Do not make the laboratory an overloaded sensory environment.
- Have well-placed and clearly labelled equipment.
- Ensure equipment is appropriately adapted to the needs of pupils.
- Place furniture carefully.
- Make good use of wall colour and displays.
- Be clear about asking questions.
- Use a range of strategies to develop communication skills.
- Use small-staged practical work to develop practical skills.
- Use small groups and partners to develop oral skills.
- Link with the mathematics faculty to determine how, and when, mathematical concepts are taught.
- Use technology to allow pupils to access the curriculum more effectively by developing information gathering skills and methods of recording of ideas.

Science should be sensory, interactive, stimulating and fun for everyone. With understanding and forward planning, science teachers can create an inclusive environment that caters to all pupils.

3　Teaching and learning

It is the last lesson of the day. The Year 7 group coming into the laboratory have just had PE, and some of them are late. You want them to design and carry out an investigation into which natural materials would make the most suitable indicator. The laboratory is hot, even with the windows open, and there are only five mortar and pestles available for the whole class. After 15 minutes of interruptions you realise they are unsure about what you want them to do; those who arrived first are bored of hearing the same instructions for the fifth time. By the end of the lesson fewer than half the class have successfully made and tested their indicator. To compound the issue, you then spend the half hour immediately after the lesson cleaning red cabbage and beetroot out of the sinks.

Some aspects of this situation are out of the hands of the science teacher – the time of day, the weather and the lesson immediately prior to yours are definitely out of your control. However, there are things that you can change which will increase the chances of your lesson having a successful outcome. Communication with colleagues when pupils consistently arrive late is important, planning and ordering apparatus in advance to avoid clashes can help and thinking of alternative methods of presenting the instructions can prove to be useful. Thinking about how the pupils can pack away their apparatus can pay dividends: a bucket for certain waste materials, appointing monitors to oversee certain aspects of the clearing away and establishing routes can all help.

Being flexible enough to change the task when you realise things are going badly wrong is an important skill to develop. As a teacher you need to develop activities which will lead to effective learning. Kyriacou writes on this subject:

> The essence of effective teaching lies in the ability of the teacher to set up a learning experience which brings about the desired educational outcomes. For this to take place, each pupil must be engaged in the activity of learning.
>
> (Kyriacou 1997: 21)

Although this statement is generic to all teaching, it is especially important to consider the links between learning – and the teaching which facilitates this – when planning work for pupils with SEND. Many of the ideas presented in this chapter apply to all science lessons with groups of all abilities but are particularly pertinent when considering classes with pupils with SEND.

The way a lesson is structured can have a big effect on the outcome. There should not be a formulaic approach to teaching where every lesson has the same structure come what may. What this chapter hopes to achieve is to share a series of possible issues to consider when planning the lesson. These are tried and tested ways of motivating the pupils whatever their attainment – some of these techniques might even work for the last lesson on a Friday immediately after PE!

This chapter is ordered around a possible lesson structure, and this structure consists of:

- An entry activity
- Sharing of objectives and learning outcomes
- An engagement activity or starter
- The main part of the lesson
- A plenary

This is an extension of the much-talked-about 'three-part lesson'. However, it is not a structure which would apply in every circumstance; it is meant to be flexible. There are many issues to be considered in the 'main' part of the lesson.

Entry activities

There are many reasons why the members of a class might arrive in dribs and drabs, not least because they have just had PE and take differing amounts of time to get dressed. For some pupils, particularly those with social, emotional and mental health (SEMH) issues or with ADHD (attention deficit hyperactivity disorder), the last thing you want is to give them time with no meaningful task, just sitting waiting for the last one to arrive. For all pupils, lesson time is valuable, and the sooner you can engage the pupils with learning activities the more productive the lesson will be.

Entry activities can come in many forms, but the main uniting factor is that they engage the pupils in a task they can undertake immediately on entry without the need for lengthy instructions from the teacher. This could be a valuable time for pupils to respond to feedback from their homework. Often in marking books you will make comments that the pupils should respond to, for example: 'Add arrows to this diagram to show the effect of friction' or 'Use the idea of particles moving faster when they are hotter to explain why the sugar dissolves faster in the hotter water'. These are formative comments the pupils could respond to immediately on entering the room and collecting their books.

This could also be an opportunity for the pupils to engage with an activity which links back to the previous lesson. A word search or anagram exercise to revise the key vocabulary thus far in the unit can help some pupils make important links. An activity where the pupils draw or label a diagram to show an element of their learning from the previous lesson could also provide valuable insights into how well the outcomes from the previous lesson have been embedded.

Learning objectives and learning outcomes

It is all too easy to teach our favourite lessons, particularly practicals, without considering how well these match the learning objectives. For example, is an experiment where the pupils scrape the inside of their mouth to make a slide of cheek cells really the best way of teaching about the structure of animal cells? Most of the pupils are not looking at animal cells but rather a bit of their breakfast anyway! This can lead to big misconceptions.

By considering the lesson objective carefully, it is easier to match the learning activities to this objective and to differentiate outcomes so that every pupil has a chance of success. The starting point for developing the objective is often some form of published curriculum; this could be the National Curriculum or an examination syllabus. The first statement in the current National Curriculum for Science at KS3 reads: 'Pupils should be taught about cells as the fundamental unit of living organisms, including how to observe, interpret and record cell structure using a light microscope'. This contains too much content for most pupils to cover in one lesson, and it is not written in language which is easy for many to understand. This needs to be written into a suitable lesson objective, such as: 'I can describe the structure of an animal cell'. You

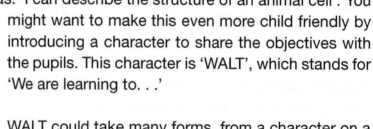

might want to make this even more child friendly by introducing a character to share the objectives with the pupils. This character is 'WALT', which stands for 'We are learning to. . .'

WALT could take many forms, from a character on a poster or interactive whiteboard slide to a glove puppet. The objective then becomes: 'We are learning to describe the structure of an animal cell'.

This does not, however, tell the pupils what they have to do to be successful – this is where we need to use learning outcomes. The learning outcomes for the lesson tell the pupils what they have to do to be successful. This is where you can introduce differentiation, so that there are outcomes at different levels.

Mechanisms that are easy to use are:

- All, Most and Some

or

- Must, Should and Could

You might want to introduce another character, called 'WILF', which stands for 'What I'm looking for. . .' So, the learning outcomes for the lesson on animal cells might be:

What I'm looking for is that. . .

- *All* of you will label a diagram to show the different parts of an animal cell.
- *Most* of you will describe the function of each of these parts.
- *Some* of you can explain why the cell membrane is not completely watertight.

These outcomes are in order of cognitive demand. Labelling is something achievable to all pupils; some will be able to draw their own diagram and label it whilst others (with SEND) might need the further support of a prepared diagram and labels. Describing is then a higher-order outcome, which most pupils in Year 7 should be able to do. Explaining 'why' represents the highest level of demand for this lesson and might be an extension activity aimed at the higher attainers.

The objectives and outcomes for a lesson are a bit like the rings on an archery target. The objective is the outer ring, and everything in the lesson falls within this. The *All* outcome is the next ring, followed by the *Most*, and then the *Some* outcome is the bull's-eye – when the pupils hit this their learning really is at the centre of where you would want it to be.

Objectives and outcomes don't have to be based on knowledge and understanding – they could be based on investigation skills or on learning skills. However, you do not want to confuse the pupils with too many. One knowledge and understanding–based objective and one investigation skills–based objective is plenty. Each of these can then have up to three differentiated learning outcomes.

It should not be necessary to ask pupils with SEND to copy learning objectives into their books. For some pupils, this will be the most writing they can manage in a lesson, and copying from the board in itself can be problematic. Should school policy dictate that learning objectives are required in books, consider providing these for pupils so that they can stick them into their books. (It's possible to use sticky-backed address labels for this, printed out in a sheet for each pupil to take one; this is an activity a TA could reasonably be tasked with.)

Starters

There has been much debate about whether a starter activity should be used before or after sharing the objectives and outcomes. There is no one simple answer to this. It is good practice to share the objectives and outcomes first, otherwise the pupils are wandering aimlessly through the starter without an outcome to head towards. However, the starter can be the place to introduce key vocabulary, and the objective might not make sense without this. Alternatively, you might want to engage the pupils in a bit of thought around a topic, and this then might lead into the development of the objective.

A starter is more than just an introduction to the lesson; it is about engaging the pupils in thought to try to stimulate ideas and an interest in the next part of the lesson. The starter is also a good place to elicit the pupils' ideas and misconceptions about the topic of the lesson. It is therefore an important step in the learning process. A well-selected starter can help many pupils with SEND make an initial step in their learning which will make the main part of the lesson more accessible.

A starter which stimulates discussion can be usefully employed for some lessons. A picture or photograph related to the topic can provide such a stimulus. For example, a lesson on forces might have a picture of a tug-of-war match, together with a list of key words: the pupils then have to describe the picture using as many of the key words as possible. There is an example of this type of starter in Appendix 3.1. A lesson on diffusion might start with a demonstration of a gas jar of bromine being exposed to a gas jar of air: the pupils then need to describe and explain what is happening to the brown colour of the bromine.

Some of the scientific vocabulary can be confusing enough for many pupils, but particularly so for pupils with SEND. Starter sessions can address the technical vocabulary which will be used in the lesson. A lesson on photosynthesis might start with the pupils brainstorming, or even using dictionaries to look up, as many words as possible using the prefix 'photo-'. They could then be asked to find a link between these words, leading to the idea of light. This will then help them understand the process of photosynthesis better.

Card sorts provide a good mechanism for eliciting pupils' ideas and misconceptions. In a lesson on drugs, pupils could be asked to sort cards of different drugs to demonstrate their understanding of the legality and addictiveness of these drugs. This type of activity is particularly powerful when revisited at the end of the lesson to see how the pupils' ideas have moved forward.

Concept Cartoons (see Resources section) are a valuable resource to stimulate discussions in class and can be accessed at a range of levels for pupils. Again, these can be used to support the acquisition of appropriate scientific vocabulary.

The main part of the lesson

Use of DART activities

DART stands for Directed Activity Related to Text and is a useful tool to support pupils in translating text into other forms and thus particularly appropriate for many pupils with SEN. There are many different types of DART activity; we will deal with some of the main ones here.

Cloze procedures

Probably the best known of all DART activities is the cloze procedure, which usually consists of a passage of text with key words missing, and the pupils have to then use either their knowledge of the topic or another passage of text to fill in these missing words. Different levels of support can be given; for example, the missing words can be in a box at the top so that the pupils can cross these off as they complete the task, or dashes can replace the missing words to indicate the number of letters. The following example shows part of a cloze exercise related to energy transfer in food chains:

All of the energy in a food chain originally comes from the _ _ _.

This energy is captured by plants through the process of _ _ _ _ _ _ _ _ _ _.

The plant is called the _ _ _ _ _ _ _ _.

Some animals eat only plants; they are called primary _ _ _ _ _ _ _ _ _

When these animals eat the plants the _ _ _ _ _ _ is transferred to them.

Great care should be taken in the use of cloze activities. These often provide little challenge; pupils can sometimes guess the words to fill the gaps with little comprehension of the whole text. Cloze activities are probably best used in combination with other activities but not as the sole mechanism for learning.

There is an example of a cloze activity on the accompanying website at www.routledge.com/9781138209053.

Text marking

Text marking provides a relatively straightforward activity which in its simplest form avoids the need for any detailed passages of writing. This usually involves pupils being given a passage of text, and they underline parts of it that are related to different issues. For example, in a lesson on global warming, the pupils might be given a newspaper article and asked to mark it in the following ways:

- Underline in blue any part of the text which provides evidence that the Earth is warming up.
- Underline in red any part of the text which gives the causes of this warming up.
- Underline in green any steps being taken to try to reduce this warming up.

This can lead into the pupils using the parts of the text they have marked to produce their own piece of writing, possibly in a different format or genre, around the same topic. Care should be taken with the choice for the original piece of text – newspaper articles in their original form may not be accessible to all pupils. These might, therefore, need to be translated into a simpler form of text, and the use of the first person can be powerful in making text more accessible. A teaching assistant may take on this function as part of the support role.

A quick assessment of the reading level of a piece of text can be obtained using the SMOG formula (see Appendix 3.2).

Diagram and text completion

Diagram completion or labelling can provide an effective way of checking pupil understanding of a passage of text and giving them a useful way of recording the main points from it. The pupils are given a passage of text and asked to use it to label or complete a diagram. For example, they might be given a passage on the structure of plant cells and might use this to label a diagram showing the different parts of a plant cell. You might combine this activity with text marking to provide an interim step to make this activity more accessible.

Text completion involves giving the pupils the start to a sentence or paragraph and then asking them to complete it. For example, when studying electrical circuits, you might ask them to complete a passage of text which starts:

In our first circuit, the bulb was lit because. . .

In our second circuit, the two bulbs were dim because. . .

Clearly, text completion can be set at a relatively high level of demand, as to complete the prior sentences fully would require an understanding of complete circuits and of current being shared between bulbs. Pupils might need two or three attempts at these to include enough detail.

Text matching

Text matching is similar to text completion but made easier by the fact that the second part of the sentence is provided. This means that rather than having to think of the reasons, the pupils just need to identify the correct option. So, in a text matching exercise which includes the two sentence starters listed earlier, among the sentence endings might be:

. . . there is a complete circuit, with no gaps in it.

. . . the electric current from the cell is shared between the two bulbs.

Sentence ordering

Sentence ordering is an exercise which can be used to help pupils make sense of a passage of text. The passage is divided up into sentences, and the pupils are then presented with these as a series of cards which they need to place into the correct order. For example, when studying solar eclipses, the pupils could be given sentences which describe a viewer's observations during an eclipse and be asked to place these into chronological order. This exercise might be taken to the next level by asking the pupils to describe why these phenomena were observed at each point in terms of the relative positions of the three bodies involved.

True/false exercises

Maybe one of the simplest forms of DART exercise is a true/false exercise. Pupils are given a series of statements, and they simply have to state whether these are true or false. This could be for series of statements about the function of specialised plant cells, for example. In other examples where the evidence is less clear-cut, the pupils might be asked to decide whether they agree or disagree, and this could then lead into discussions about the topic.

Word puzzles

There are various forms of word puzzle that can be used. The most common are crosswords and word searches, which can be particularly useful in developing pupils' recognition of key vocabulary. A crossword of circuit symbols could be used where the pupils are given the symbols as the clues and have to write the names in the crossword grid. A word search of different types of food could be given to the pupils: not only could they identify the words, but they could colour-code the different food groups. For example, they could shade all the foods which are a good source of protein in red.

These are just some of the forms of the DART approach. It is important to try to match the form of activity to the topic and to the pupils so they can achieve success. It is also important that you use a mix of different activities to provide variety; if you gave out a cloze exercise every lesson the pupils would soon become bored.

Developing ideas

It is important to consider which part of the lesson contains the stage where the pupils develop their ideas most. In a practical lesson this is often the stage where the pupils write their conclusions. Traditionally, we ask pupils to write a two-paragraph conclusion, one describing the pattern and giving the evidence for this, the second explaining these observations in terms of the scientific ideas. This approach works well for pupils with highly developed linguistic abilities but less well for the others. We could at this stage give the pupils a range of options to present their ideas, such as bullet-pointed lists, concept maps, diagrams and maybe even discussing their ideas in a group. These all require very different skills, and we cannot expect pupils to use these straight away – they need to experience and learn each of these techniques and then develop the one(s) which work best for them. We do, however, need to bear in mind that sometimes the pupils will have to present their ideas as two paragraphs of text, for example in terminal exams, so occasionally we do need to teach this skill and let them practise it.

Modelling

Science is full of models, be they physical models or intellectual ones. All too often we present a model as fact, often confusing pupils either with this initial model or later when we have to replace it with a more sophisticated one. We need at every stage to share with the pupils what we are doing in terms of the models and to consider their limitations. Let us consider how we might develop a model of particles as an example:

Initial model – marbles in a tray, to consider how particles move compared with their internal energy.

Second model – use of coloured polystyrene balls to represent atoms, joining two or more together to form molecules.

Third model – use of particle model kits to illustrate the number of bonds each atom can form and to develop molecular formulae.

Final model – some pupils might go on and consider electron orbits in shells, then refine this to consider 'p' and 's' shells, etc. If they really take their scientific studies to the highest levels, they might consider the orbits in terms of probability of where the electrons might lie and even consider wave–particle duality.

None of these models gives an exact description of how particles appear and behave. Each one is, however, a 'good enough' model at each stage in the pupils' cognitive development. It is therefore important to treat the models as such. For some pupils with SEND models work well: they make a theoretical idea such as particles more tangible and concrete. For other pupils, however, the model becomes the concept, and therefore particles might be made of glass with coloured hits in the middle and be the size of marbles. It is therefore more important for teaching pupils with SEND than for teaching most others to consider which models to use and when to use them. For some pupils, such as those with ASD, this type of physical model can help them grasp abstract concepts.

Similar considerations need to be made with physical models. Typical home-work might be to make a model of a cell of your choice. These models will then be displayed, a great activity for pupils with highly developed bodily kin-aesthetic and spatial intelligences. However, the problem is in deciding on the best ones. For example, a plastic bag filled with water with a coloured marble floating in it might look good as an animal cell, but this can lead to misconcep-tions, in this case particularly that the cell membrane is impermeable. On the other hand, a teabag which has been slit open, a Smartie placed inside and then sewn back together might not look very attractive but better represents the semi-permeable nature of the cell membrane. In using physical models, therefore, it is important to consider their limitations as well as ways in which they are good at representing reality. Care also needs to be taken that the model does not replace the reality for some pupils with SEND.

Working Scientifically

Practical work is an essential feature of good science teaching. The aim of science is to find explanations that are supported by evidence for the events and phenomena of the natural world. So teaching science involves 'showing' students things, or putting them into situations where they can see things for themselves. Simply 'telling' them is unlikely to work. Practical work also gives students a sense of what is distinctive about science as a 'way of knowing' about the world.

(Millar 2009)

Investigation skills form the backbone of scientific discovery: in teaching these we are equipping the pupils to be real scientists and to give them the facility to solve their own scientific problems. All too often we assume that the pupils acquire the skills by undertaking investigations, and it is less usual for the individual investigation skills to be taught. This is of particular importance when teaching some pupils with SEND for whom small steps in developing learning and skills is the best approach.

It is important to give the pupils ownership of the investigation and to relate this to everyday life. If you introduce the investigation by simply telling the class that they are going to investigate how the temperature of the water affects how much sugar will dissolve in it, they are not performing their own investigation; they are performing yours. Planning posters can be useful here. By starting with an open question, such as, 'What affects sugar dissolving?' the pupils can suggest and develop their own ideas. These ideas might be many and varied: they might well include temperature but might also include other factors such as volume, size of grain, agitation and solvent.

Other investigation skills are best taught outside of the whole investigation context. Plotting graphs can be a long and tedious task for some pupils; if this is part of the investigation process it can mean that the investigation can last for a long time. Practice at graph plotting skills is important, as is the decision about when is the right time to move pupils from bar charts to line graphs. Tools such as prepared axes, marked with the appropriate values, can make the first steps in graph plotting easier to take. This means the pupils can focus on plotting the points accurately first and develop this skill before moving on to selecting the correct scale for the axes.

Some pupils will have particular difficulty with writing conclusions, especially if this involves interpreting graphs. Looking at a graph and seeing the pattern it is displaying is an advanced skill and is definitely an abstract skill. Some pupils will find this easier if the graphs are translated back into numbers; for example, when the temperature was 30 degrees Celsius, three spoonfuls dissolved, but when the temperature rose to 60 degrees Celsius, five spoonfuls dissolved. Others might find pictorial representations of the graph more useful, for example comparing the line of the graph to a hill they have to climb so they have to describe what it would be like to climb the hill at various stages.

The main learning point for an experiment or investigation is often developed in the concluding stage. There is often little to be learned from 'writing up' an experiment. This is a task to be used sparingly as it can provide real barriers to many pupils and can become tedious for others. When you do want to develop the skill of describing a practical, this can be particularly difficult for pupils with dyslexia/dyspraxia who find sequencing and organising their work difficult. These pupils could benefit from a series of cards which they have to put into the correct order to help remind them of how they undertook the investigation.

Source: © Fox Lane Photography

For other pupils, where writing is a real barrier to learning, a voice recorder can be employed, and they can relay their ideas verbally into this.

Health and safety are important issues in the laboratory. Teaching the lesson in small units will help keep pupils focused. Asking pupils to make risk assessments of the practical work before it is undertaken, either written or verbal, will also emphasise the need to consider safety.

Plenaries

Evidence suggests that the plenary is the least effective part of the lesson for many teachers; it is often just a quick recap at the end of the lesson. It could, however, be argued that the plenary is the most important part of the lesson and that rather than a quick two-minute recap, a longer period is needed. This has implications for the rest of the lesson and for your planning as a teacher – you need to ensure that you leave enough time for an effective plenary.

The main function of the plenary is for assessment, not just to inform the teacher but also to inform the pupils. At the start of the lesson you shared some learning outcomes with the pupils, and it is in the plenary where the pupils get the opportunity to measure themselves against these outcomes. There are various techniques for doing this. One of the least effective techniques is to ask a few questions of the class as a whole and allow the six pupils who put their hands up to answer. This does not tell you or the majority of the pupils how their learning has progressed, only the six who try to answer. Some pupils with SEND are reticent to attempt to answer questions in front of the whole class, and thus more interactive techniques are needed.

Yes/No cards are useful for eliciting whole-class responses. The word 'Yes' can be printed on red paper, the word 'No' on green paper, and these can then be laminated back to back. Questions relating to the lesson can then be asked and the pupils respond 'Yes' or 'No' by holding up their cards. This gets instant feedback from the whole class, and the use of colours helps you spot any different responses quickly. The use of follow-up questions to individuals will then help you gain some understanding of why they have responded in this way.

Most science departments have at least one set of mini whiteboards, about A4 size, with dry-wipe marker pens. These open up a whole vista of activities with which you can elicit whole-class responses. For example, in a lesson where the objective has been based around drawing distance/time graphs, the pupils could use these whiteboards to sketch graphs as you tell them a story of your journey to school. In a lesson on cells, you might want the pupils to draw and label an animal cell on the whiteboards. In a lesson on forces, you might ask the class to draw a picture of a car travelling at 70 mph and draw all the forces acting on it. It can be surprising how quickly a glance around the room at these boards being held up gives you an idea of the pupils' understanding. These whiteboards can be particularly successful with some pupils with SEND: the fact that they know they are going to rub out their answer, rather than having it appear forever in their exercise books, allows them to be more confident and to have a go.

Pupils of all ages enjoy games, and this can be exploited in the plenary. If you want to ask the pupils a series of multiple-choice questions, this could be dressed up as a 'Who Wants to Be a Millionaire?' type game – a lot more fun. A grid of letters can be displayed with words associated with the lesson content, and this could then become a 'Blockbusters' type game. Other games can be developed which can be played in groups. For example, in a lesson on the elements, the pupils could play dominoes, where the dominoes have the name of an element on one side and the symbol for this element on the other.

Remember the card sorts mentioned in the starters? If these are revisited in the plenary, it helps you and the pupils identify where their learning has moved forward. In the card sorts on drugs, they might have sorted the cards into 'Legal', 'Illegal' and 'Not sure'. After the main part of the lesson they may want to add another category, 'Controlled', and some of the drugs which might have been in other categories can now be moved into this one, demonstrating new understanding.

Performing a plenary is not quite the end of the story. When the lesson has ended, you need a few moments to reflect on the pupils' learning and to decide where to go next. If the objective of the lesson was for the pupils to accurately define the terms 'atom' and 'element' and in a plenary the pupils have clearly shown they do not have an understanding of these two terms, then there is no way you can go on to the next lesson on molecules and compounds. Most schemes of work contain a series of lessons which contain ideas which build on each other. It is not good practice to mindlessly teach lesson 1, followed by lesson 2, followed by lesson 3, and so on, unless the pupils have grasped the ideas from the previous lesson. You might need to revisit the objective with a different activity to try to move the pupils' learning forward.

Assessment for learning

Throughout the lesson it is important to give pupils opportunities to use self-assessment techniques so they can monitor and develop their own learning. There are a range of techniques that can be used, from using 'traffic light' cards to show how confident pupils are in completing the task they have been set, to self-evaluation during the plenary, commenting how well they feel they have met the success criteria, for example. This gives you as the teacher the chance to see how well pupils think they have done with the topic at hand and the opportunity to modify future planning if it appears more time needs to be spent on certain concepts.

For pupils with SEND it might be helpful to provide a self-assessment sheet which has been pre-populated with key learning objectives from the topic.

Use of homework

Before setting homework, you need to consider such questions as, 'Is this homework really appropriate for this group?' and 'What benefit will these pupils gain from undertaking this piece of homework?' For some pupils routine is important, so if homework is regularly set on a certain night of the week, it may be best to stick to this. There are positive reasons to set homework – it can be used to:

- Develop skills used in the lesson
- Reinforce some of the ideas from the lesson
- Test knowledge gained
- Develop key vocabulary
- Give opportunities for independent research
- Allow pupils time to plan and carry out surveys
- Put the learning into context in the home
- Allow the application of ideas to new situations by using problem-solving skills

Homework can become a real barrier and for some an area of failure. If a pupil is consistently not completing homework and getting into trouble the following lesson, this barrier to learning will then overflow into lesson time. Be aware that some pupils with ASD compartmentalise their lives so that school work is not done at home, meaning they will struggle to complete homework and may get into trouble for this. It might be necessary to arrange homework catch-up sessions, either as a department or in collaboration with the school SEND department. Other pupils may achieve a high level of success within the lesson, but if inappropriate homework is set this might temper that success. It is therefore important to set differentiated homework, especially for those pupils who will not have any support at home. For pupils with disabilities which make them more tired than most, you need to consider the amount of homework with which they have to cope. In a class which contains pupils with SEND, it is also important to consider when to set the homework; for example, if you set this in the last two minutes of the lesson (as many teachers do), do these pupils have time to record what they have to do and check if they do not understand?

Appendix 3.3 gives examples of different styles of homework that could be used with pupils with varying special needs. One considers key words; the second is a research technique that could be used; the third looks at writing an experimental report.

Conclusion

If there were one simple answer to how to teach science as effectively as possible, someone would have discovered it by now and would probably have retired on the profits. However, structuring your lessons carefully and planning these around the objectives will certainly get you on the right track. Variety is also important. Most lessons can be broken down into learning episodes, and this is particularly important when teaching pupils with SEND. Short, sharp activities are invariably better than long, drawn-out ones. Appendix 3.4 can be used and shared with other teachers as a reminder of the main principles of lesson planning.

Every child and every class is different, and it is not possible to pull standard lessons off the shelf and assume they will work. You need to consider how to modify certain tasks for certain pupils and present an appropriate level of challenge to move their learning forward, but at the same time any task must not be so difficult that it can only result in failure. To quote Sotto (1997):

> To teach in a way which takes account of the way people learn requires systematic study of how they learn followed by a great many struggles to translate such study into effective practice.

4 Monitoring and assessment

The Year 7 group is working on food chains and webs. One of the pupils, Jasmine, is on a dual placement from a special school and has significant cognitive difficulties; she has very limited verbal communication. Another pupil, Anna, asks for paper and glue. She has decided to make the pictures provided into a booklet for Jasmine to take back to her school. Jasmine communicates non-verbally about which pictures she has selected. This was not part of the original plan, but the teacher can see that a lot of learning is taking place. Initial concerns have been allayed because even without verbal communication these pupils can interact and learn, albeit on different levels. This may be an occasion when you have to look at the learning beyond the work done and see the social progress made by the group working together. The pupil with special needs has demonstrated basic understanding of food chains, and Anna has been able to strengthen her understanding by virtue of having to help Jasmine and reinforce the teacher's input.

It is important for science teachers to consider what they need to monitor and how monitoring and assessments are performed.

Pupils should have a teacher assessment for science at the end of the primary phase, and their information should be available for use within departments (although it is current practice for pupils to be grouped into two categories – 'working at' and 'did not meet' the expected standards).

Within the National Curriculum there is a programme of study setting out the content that needs to be taught. At key stage 4, most pupils follow a syllabus which is the examination board's interpretation of the National Curriculum. Specifications now set out assessment objectives so teachers can consider the best course for their pupils, and it is important to consider these in the light of pupils' individual needs. Entry-level qualifications are more appropriate for some pupils, whilst others can achieve well at GCSE (or equivalent) with special dispensations such as extra time or the services of an amanuensis.

If you have pupils who fall into this category, it is important to liaise with the SENCO as early as possible because there is a requirement for a specialist assessor to provide a report to support the application. (It is also important to check whether any special arrangements need to be applied for in advance; *Access Arrangements, Reasonable Adjustments and Special Consideration* outlines these arrangements and is sent to every school – copies are available from JCQ.)

Target setting

Target setting can be particularly useful for pupils with SEND who may well be outside the target group of pupils achieving age-related expectations at the end of key stage 3 and whose learning objectives may therefore be different from the majority in the class. It is important to see where the pupil is currently before 'SMART' targets for improvement can be set. These are:

- **S**pecific
- **M**easurable
- **A**ttainable
- **R**elevant
- **T**ime targeted

This approach may relate to practical work, such as being able to light a Bunsen burner independently. Other examples of SMART targets would be to describe a fair test when writing a plan for an experiment, plotting up to five points on a graph accurately or writing a risk assessment for an experiment they have to perform during a lesson. Meaningful SMART targets can only be set if the science teacher possesses a sound grasp of each pupil's current attainment.

Group education plans can be used to set targets for pupils with similar learning needs, but individual targets obviously can be tailored more carefully and therefore potentially can be more effective. Where pupils are known to the SEND support team, and possibly have an Education Health and Care Plan, the science teacher may be asked to contribute appropriate targets. Whatever method is used by the science faculty, it is important to communicate the targets to the pupils and revisit them regularly. For pupils with a special educational need, the target level needs to be discussed with them sensitively, either by their science teacher or by the teaching assistant. It is important to make sure the pupils understand precisely what is expected of them.

If they are to have relevance to the pupil, targets must also be monitored and reviewed, giving the pupil regular and specific feedback. This can be of particular value when a pupil with an EHC plan has an annual review or when targets are being reviewed. Up-to-date information on how pupils are progressing towards their target is important for the SENCO in such situations.

Some schools carry out interim progress reviews and report to parents half-yearly. If the pupil with special needs is not meeting the target for the whole group, problems may arise at the school monitoring stage. Science staff who report back to heads of year or senior staff need to be clear how progress is monitored. There is a danger that pupils are regarded as underachieving because they may not have the same target as the rest of the group. In fact, the truth could be that they are making good progress towards their individual target and even making progress at a faster rate than other pupils.

Within the faculty it is useful to have a standard letter that can be sent to parents if pupils have made good progress, with some facility for individual teacher comment. For pupils with SEND, small improvements may be recorded and reported to parents outside the normal contact methods.

It is important to note these four principles as set out in the statutory inclusion statement (National Curriculum Framework 2015). These are:

- Teachers should set high expectations for every pupil. . . They have an even greater obligation to plan lessons for pupils who have low levels of prior attainment or come from disadvantaged backgrounds. Teachers should use appropriate assessment to set targets which are deliberately ambitious.
- Teachers should take account of their duties under equal opportunities legislation that covers race, disability, sex, religion or belief, sexual orientation, pregnancy and maternity and gender reassignment.
- A wide range of pupils have SEND, many of whom also have disabilities. Lessons should be planned to ensure there are no barriers to every pupil achieving.
- With the right teaching, that recognises their individual needs, many disabled pupils may have little need for additional resources beyond the aids which they use as part of their daily life. Teachers must plan lessons so that these pupils can study every national curriculum subject. Potential areas of difficulty should be identified and addressed at the outset of work.

Choosing the right course

It is always helpful to review the course each year and consider if it is meeting the needs of all your pupils. If you decide to change, the first decision at key stage 3 is whether you are going to write your own course or buy a ready-made package.

The advantage of writing your own course is that you can tailor it to suit your own needs in terms of it being appropriate for the pupils you teach. You can build in progression of understanding and of skills learned and use activities to suit teacher expertise and resources available.

The advantage of a published scheme is that it generally has built-in National Curriculum links and assessment procedures. The best schemes provide a toolkit of ideas and resources which give the teacher the opportunity to select the most appropriate activities to suit the needs of the class. Rather than being prescriptive, these will suggest possible routes through the curriculum to meet different needs. (Usually, however, there will still be a need for further differentiation for some pupils.) Be wary of published material that is too prescriptive and inflexible.

Whichever course of action is taken, time will be required to write or adapt the course to suit the needs of the faculty. Even a bought package will require some adaptations, and time will be needed to familiarise everyone within the faculty on how it is administered.

At key stage 4, it is important to choose the course most suitable for the pupils. Some pupils will be able to cope with the rigours of a double GCSE with some support such as a computer, an adult to give support within the classroom or as an amanuensis, adapted apparatus or a signer. It is important to check the degree of assistance allowed by the examination board chosen and if they require any information. This needs to be clarified preferably before embarking on the course. Others will succeed best doing an alternative such as OCR Nationals and others with an entry-level course. Consideration needs to be given as to whether an academic or vocational course is more appropriate.

Measuring progress

Why do we need to assess progress? Knowing the standard attained by the pupil is essential for the teacher when planning future work and reporting back to parents. It may also be required by the SEND department when they have to hold annual reviews or report back to outside agencies. It is useful for pupils to be able to review their own progress and can be a way of raising their self-esteem. There are also times when schools have to report back to the government regarding the progress made at the end of the key stage. Formal assessment of a pupil's attainment can only be made at the end of a key stage when the full breadth of the curriculum has been covered. The pupil's progress can, however, be measured during a topic and used to help in the target-setting process.

Some courses bought as packages may have end-of-unit tests provided. These are valuable, but it is also good practice to use a variety of assessment methods rather than just an end-of-unit test in order to make adaptations to the unit to ensure all pupils understand the work. It is poor teaching practice if scientific concepts are introduced without previous ones being understood. The plenary session is a useful method by which to assess the progress made during a lesson.

Asking the teaching assistant at the end of the lesson if the particular pupils they have been working with have grasped the concepts can be useful. They may also provide valuable information about others within the group and how they have responded during the lesson.

At both key stage 3 and key stage 4 practical work needs to be assessed using appropriate feedback to the pupils, showing that, for instance, if they give scientific reasons for their analysis their marks are increased. This method of marking, if communicated to the pupils, gives them feedback and allows them to develop their skills as they know what is expected the next time they complete the same type of work.

Here are some further ideas that are useful when assessing pupils with a special educational need:

- For those with poor literacy skills, at key stage 3 when looking at renewable fuels, they could have pictures with pre-prepared text so they could stick the pictures and correct writing into their books. This indicates their understanding and not their writing skill.
- Using a voice recorder for homework can be a useful alternative to writing down results. For instance, at key stage 4 when writing the results for an experiment after testing urine (obviously artificial; cold tea with chemicals added is a wonderful substitute!), pupils could record their findings and also explain their conclusion. If it is necessary for them to have notes, you could then photocopy someone else's notes for them because you know they understand the science of how kidneys function.
- Listening to pupils talking among themselves about the work gives an insight into individual understanding. This can be done in formal or informal settings. Again, if you are considering fuels at key stage 3, by setting up a class debate with every pupil having a part to play it is possible to assess the progress of pupils with SEND. Be sure to allow sufficient planning and rehearsal time – providing a speaking frame can also be useful.
- Another useful method when assessing progress could be to ask everyone in the class to write a mnemonic. The obvious use of a mnemonic is when remembering the colours of the spectrum or the order of the planets, but they can be used equally successfully for remembering other specific details. Often, the pupils will suggest them as a way of remembering facts – if they get the mnemonic right you know instantly whether they have grasped a particular concept or fact.

- The use of simple tunes is another way pupils can show their understanding. Key stage 4 work about electrical circuits has some possibilities. If they put *resistance equals voltage divided by current* to a simple or popular tune, such as one for an advertisement, and they then either record them or repeat them next lesson, it is easier for pupils to remember and apply such concepts.
- As the pupils complete practical work, taking photographs of them can be valuable. Also making and watching a video so they can see how they perform a particular experiment can be a valuable tool, although there is the issue of confidentiality and written permission is required to photograph or film pupils. When developing the skill of using a measuring cylinder at key stage 3, a teaching aid can be created by photographing pupils using one to point out any mistakes (such as not getting their eye level with the meniscus or tipping the measuring cylinder).

Source: © Fox Lane Photography

- Using True/False or Yes/No cards as a whole group to answer simple questions shows the level of understanding of scientific concepts within a group. Noticing who is looking around and copying others indicates how confident they are and where their knowledge is lacking. It is important to use follow-up questions such as, 'What reasons do you have for answering False to that question?' This can be a useful starter or plenary, especially at key stage 3. For example, it can be used to test their understanding of particles and how they behave in solids, liquids and gases.
- For assessment to be of value there needs to be feedback given to the pupils. Again, the method may vary from speaking individually with a pupil to asking the whole group. This is a valuable method after group presentations and can lead to raising the self-esteem of pupils if the feedback is constructive.

Whatever method is employed, the pupils need to feel it is a fair process, and it is important to link the feedback, either verbal or written, to the learning objectives set at the outset of the lesson. For example, if the learning objective is to understand displacement reactions and the pupil has obviously not understood that they are dependent on the reactivity of the metals used, it is not acceptable just to indicate the pupil's answers are wrong. The pupil also needs to know that the more reactive metal displaces the less reactive metal; without this knowledge he or she will never understand displacement reactions.

Formally recording progress also needs consideration. When marking tests, writing the mark alone can be unhelpful. Giving comments which relate to progress against individual targets is far more supportive, as is helpful advice about exactly how to do better next time. The pupils then know how they are performing and where improvements need to be made. For instance, they may have just completed a unit containing ideas about photosynthesis and their test indicates they have failed to understand that oxygen is given off as a by-product of the reaction. Their next unit may contain work about respiration, and by having the teacher's comment about oxygen, they will find the next unit easier to understand.

How do teachers record the results? Are these fed back to a centrally held database for the faculty? This is an excellent way of tracking the progress of pupils: it allows comparisons between individual pupils and allows tracking of pupils' individual progress over the whole of a key stage.

Completed test papers can be used to assess the quality of teaching for individual groups. Although the process takes time, the information that it gives to the teacher or science department is invaluable.

Table 4.1 Table to help monitor test results for a group

Set_____	Record of marks for end of topic test								
Name of pupil	Question number and number of marks for each question								Total number of marks (50)
	1	2	3	4	5	6	7	etc.	
	(5)	(6)	(3)	(6)	(4)	(3)	(5)		

This sort of analysis (Table 4.1) highlights the strengths and weaknesses of pupils and can be a valuable tool for the science teacher, especially when comparing pupils with a particular special need to their peers and deciding on the best course for them at key stage 4. It also allows the science teacher to report accurately to the SEND faculty.

As they are easy to set up and save on a computer, and spreadsheets can do all the calculations if required, useful information can be stored and used to monitor pupils. Other details, such as estimated grades or actual grades, could also be included. By using a standard format, a blank document can be stored and then used for a variety of record-keeping purposes and can ensure the faculty is working together. It is also useful for tracking pupils, including those with SEND, throughout a key stage. Table 4.2 shows how this might be done.

A number of useful methods can be used when recording assessments for practical work. A can-do test method can be used: if the teacher observes a pupil handling a piece of apparatus correctly, a tick is placed by their name. This helps build up a picture of their capabilities with practical work. This is particularly important if they have fine or gross motor skill problems. Taking a video of them working can also be valuable for these types of pupils, but it is important to remember that some pupils will be embarrassed or feel nervous. In such circumstances, taking videos of the whole group could make a differ-ence so they do not feel singled out. If they still find the method embarrassing, consider other methods.

A simple grid can be used when recording scientific enquiry work. For most pupils just the type of skill can be used (for example, 'using a measuring cylin-der' or 'plotting a bar chart'), but finer detail may be required to show progress for some pupils with SEND (for example, 'reading a scale in twos' or 'labelling

Table 4.2 Table to monitor the progress of pupils through a key stage

Set_____	Record of marks								Overall attainment for the year
Name of pupil	*Unit number and marks for that unit*								
	1	1	3	4	5	6	7	etc.	
	(25)	(25)	(25)	(25)	(25)	(25)	(25)		

Table 4.3 Monitoring Working Scientifically skills within a key stage

Name of pupil	*Working Scientifically practical skills*			
Title of work	Plan experiments and make predictions	Use appropriate techniques and equipment	Make and record observations and measurements	Interpret observations and evaluate the methods

given axes'), and this requires careful consideration. Table 4.3 gives one way this may be done.

By considering the nature of the task set, it may be possible to record small steps the pupil has gained. For some pupils more detailed records may be of greater value to show progression.

Recording results for pupils with poor motor skills

A Year 7 group is studying cells. They are considering plant and animal cells and are introduced to the idea that there are differences between plant and animal cells. They are provided with a labelled diagram of an animal cell and shown how to make a plant cell slide from an onion. They have previously used a microscope to look at a variety of objects to see how it can be used to give information about structure. Initially they have to write down what they would do and then carry out the experiment, recording their results.

Within the group is a pupil with cerebral palsy who finds using apparatus difficult but has a TA present. The pupil could record what he or she has been

Table 4.4 Table to monitor progress of a pupil with cerebral palsy

Name of pupil	Working Scientifically: practical skills			
Title of work	Plan experiments and make predictions	Use appropriate techniques and equipment	Make and record observations and measurements	Interpret observations and evaluate the methods
What are the differences between a plant and animal cell?	*Lists apparatus needed*	*Gives instructions to partner to make the slide accurately*	*Tells TA what to draw after viewing plant slide*	*Can clearly state how to make an improvement to the experiment*
	Sequences stages for making the slide	*Tells partner how to set up the microscope*	*Tells TA what to draw when viewing animal slide*	*Can say two differences between slides*
	Gives a safety point			

doing, in the form of photographs or voice or video recording. To support this, a sheet like Table 4.4 could be used. The TA could fill in sections, and if the pupil correctly knows how to make the slide, the TA could tick the box. By using this sort of table, small areas of improvement can be noticed and recorded.

Contributing to reviews

Many teachers in secondary schools are unaware of the detailed SEND reporting procedures within a school. However, with a greater knowledge of the reporting system for SEND pupils, the science faculty can supply key information about individual pupils. Such detailed records as mentioned earlier can be invaluable when, for example, writing a report for the SEND team for the annual review for a pupil with motor skill problems.

It is therefore helpful to have an understanding of the type of reporting system for SEND required within your school. A science teacher will be able to make a valuable contribution to annual reviews as well as targets written for specific pupils. This is where having a designated member of staff linking with the SEND department becomes useful. He or she can explain to the other science teachers the type of information required and the depth of detail to be included.

The SEND department usually has a standard form when asking teachers to report back for annual reviews and when making comments for the review of targets. This enables relevant information to be collected in a unified manner.

You may be asked throughout the year to comment about the following, depending on the purpose of the enquiry:

- How well the pupil is working towards his or her targets
- His or her positive achievements within your subject
- How your course is differentiated to suit the pupil's requirements
- How practical work is differentiated and whether adapted apparatus is used
- The way in which the support provided by the SEND department is used within the lesson
- Whether the pupil is achieving his or her curriculum target
- How he or she can make further progress within your subject
- How the pupil is coping with social skills

This is the generic information required from all subjects, but the nature of science means that useful information can be provided about their practical skills. It is possible to comment on a pupil's ability to pour from containers and the adaptations required, such as using a funnel or a piece of non-slip matting, that it would be impossible to comment about in other subjects (see Table 4.5). Simple can-do tests provide useful measures of progress and can help build pupils' confidence.

Table 4.5 Monitoring Working Scientifically skills at key stage 4

Name:	Date observed, and detail of task
Class:	
I can:	
light a Bunsen burner	
adjust a Bunsen burner to make a blue flame	
measure the volume of a liquid	
use a microscope	
heat a test tube in a flame	
find the pH of a liquid	
use a spatula	
measure the temperature of a liquid	
filter a mixture	
time how long a reaction takes	
use a retort stand	
measure the mass of an object	
set up a circuit with a bulb	
measure the current in a circuit	
measure the voltage of a cell	
count the number of beats of a pulse in a minute	

P scales

Some pupils may not be working towards age-related expectations, and P scales (performance descriptors outlining attainment before KS1 age-related expectations) can be used both to report progress and to effectively differentiate work set.

Although these are no longer statutory, they are still useful where a pupil is working below KS1 expectations. The full descriptors can be found at www. gov.uk/government/uploads/system/uploads/attachment_data/file/329911/ Performance_-_P_Scale_-_attainment_targets_for_pupils_with_special_ educational_needs.pdf.

Key stage 4

The KS4 National Curriculum Programme of Study for Science (2015) states,

> The sciences should be taught in ways that ensure students have the knowledge to enable them to develop curiosity about the natural world, insight into working scientifically and appreciation of the relevance of science to their everyday lives, so that students:
>
> - develop scientific knowledge and conceptual understanding through the specific disciplines of biology, chemistry and physics
> - develop understanding of the nature, processes and methods of science, through different types of scientific enquiry that help them to answer scientific questions about the world around them
> - develop and learn to apply observational, practical, modelling, enquiry, problem-solving skills and mathematical skills, both in the laboratory, in the field and in other environments
> - develop their ability to evaluate claims based on science through critical analysis of the methodology, evidence and conclusions, both qualitatively and quantitatively

This is a huge expectation for pupils with SEND, and care will be needed when considering which course they will follow during key stage 4. What is right for one pupil will not necessarily be right for another, and so individual pathways will need to be planned. The skills mentioned in the third and fourth bullet points will need to be practised explicitly with pupils on a regular basis. Further liaison with the mathematics department may be necessary to continue to develop the skills of individuals, and it might be useful to stage interventions in particular skills for small groups of pupils on a rotational timetable. For example, interventions could involve how to apply those observational and problem-solving skills in line with questions on exam papers, continuing working to develop particular practical techniques or practicing writing a conclusion from evidence which is pre-prepared.

Some pupils with SEND are quite capable of completing dual award science courses. Others will need some adapted materials or support. It is important to sort out the needs of the pupils and apply for any special arrangements well before the exam process begins. For other pupils, there are alternative accreditation opportunities.

Pupils at key stage 4 who operate below the age-related expectations for key stages 1 and 2 may follow courses leading to accreditation for an 'entry level in science'. Those operating higher may follow a syllabus leading to potential accreditation for a vocational qualification such as a BTEC in science. For further information, contact the awarding bodies listed here.

AQA: www.aqa.org.uk/subjects/science/gcse

Edexcel: http://qualifications.pearson.com/en/qualifications/edexcel-gcses.html

OCR: www.ocr.org.uk/qualifications/by-subject/science/

Conclusion

The science faculty may need to adapt and adjust information for the SEND department within a school for the variety of reports and assessments that have to be completed. Having one named science teacher to act as liaison with the SEND department can be especially helpful in this regard.

Assessment, if used in a positive manner with pupils with SEND, can be of great value. It is important to acknowledge and praise even the smallest achievements in order to build pupils' self-esteem and keep them motivated.

For some pupils, the smallest step represents a huge effort – teachers need to recognise this and reward accordingly.

5   Managing support

One of the main principles laid out in the Special Educational Needs and Disability Code of Practice is that:

> High quality teaching that is differentiated and personalised will meet the individual needs of the majority of children and young people. Some children and young people need educational provision that is additional to or different from this. . . . Schools and colleges must use their best endeavours to ensure that such provision is made for those who need it. Special educational provision is underpinned by high quality teaching and is compromised by anything less.
>
> (DfE 2015)

This principle has a bearing on every science faculty and their provision for pupils with SEND, especially as there is a continuing emphasis on inclusive schools. Consideration will need to be given to different support strategies and how they can be structured to meet the individual needs of pupils within the context of science lessons, particularly in light of the expectation that 'every teacher is a teacher of pupils with SEND'.

Teaching assistants are prevalent in most schools, and recent reports have suggested that their deployment is not always as effective as it might be. The Deployment and Impact of Support Staff (DISS) project looked at how TAs were deployed in schools and found that many TAs were more focused on helping pupils complete the tasks they had been given rather than helping them understand what they had been asked to learn. Additionally, it found that there was little, if any, chance for teachers and TAs to plan together, ensuring progress for all pupils. It recommended that pupils with SEND should spend more time with the teacher, while the TA supports the more able pupils, and that more work was needed in developing the pedagogical role of support staff.

The findings from the DISS project made it clear that schools need to fundamentally rethink the way they use TAs if they are to get better value from them – and help pupils. The Effective Deployment of Teaching Assistants (EDTA) project worked with schools and pairs of teachers and TAs to develop and evaluate alternative ways of using TAs that worked for schools and for pupils. As a result, it was found that teachers were more aware of their responsibilities towards pupils with SEND and worked more often with these pupils, as well as provided TAs with clearer and more detailed lesson plans.

Both of these projects show the importance of preparing TAs appropriately to support in lessons and to ensure they are deployed effectively to maximise progress for all pupils. (See Russell, Webster, Blatchford [2013] for details of the DISS project and EDTA study.)

In many secondary and middle schools, there has been a move to train TAs in specific areas of the curriculum. This moves TAs away from supporting particular pupils in all subjects to working more closely within a faculty and developing subject knowledge as well as establishing sound working relationships with subject staff. It may be more difficult to put in place where TAs are part of the support detailed in a pupil's Education, Health and Care plan, as these may specify a number of hours of support for the pupil and 'lock in' the TA to accompanying the pupil to a range of lessons. In this situation, the TA can be expected to have good knowledge of the pupils and their particular needs, but less knowledge of science.

In large secondary schools, there is likely to be a blend of these two approaches. There may also be peripatetic teachers from pupil support teams who are allocated some time to act in an advisory capacity to support the teacher, perhaps by providing yearly training sessions in how best to work with pupils with particular difficulties.

Whatever the nature of support in science lessons, it is important for the teacher to manage the learning environment and the other adults in it. The responsibility for every pupil's learning, behaviour and achievement lies with the teacher.

> It. . . is you – the teacher – who is responsible for the progress and development of pupils in your charge. The Learning Support Department can help you achieve better outcomes for pupils, but it is not for the people who work there (who are mostly TAs, let us not forget) to do your job for you.
>
> . . . the challenge to you, as a class teacher is to consider ways in which TAs can add value to your classroom duties and responsibilities. In other words, think first of all about what you should be doing to support lower-attaining pupils and those with SEN, and then use the TA in ways that help you to facilitate that.
>
> (Russell, Webster, Blatchford, 2013)

Having a clear idea of the role of TAs and what they are expected to achieve is fundamental to making the best use of their support. The work of Russell et al. (2013) provides useful guidance on issues to be considered. Additionally, the ASE has produced a journal article on the subject, 'Working with teaching assistants to support learning in secondary schools', by Jennifer Versey (www. ase.org.uk/journals/education-in-science/2006/06/218). These form a good backbone for developing the right ethos about support within the school and the science faculty.

As a faculty, it is important to look at the SEND policy once a year and if necessary ask the SENCO to attend the meeting so that any concerns can be discussed. This will enable staff to have shared objectives when teaching pupils with SEND, and there will be better continuity. It is valuable for the faculty to have their own SEND policy statement, setting out clear objectives that are annually reviewed. These could include:

- That all science teachers are responsible for meeting the needs of the pupils they teach
- Working with TAs and how they are included within the faculty
- A reminder about confidentiality
- Linking with the SEND department and where to gain information
- An update on adapted apparatus and differentiated worksheets and where to find these

(See Appendix 1.2 for more information on policy writing.)

Types of support

There are a number of ways in which a TA can provide support:

- **Support the teacher**
  If the TA works with individual pupils on a regular basis, she/he is likely to know the sort of difficulties which might be encountered in science lessons – and how to avoid or overcome them. The TA could suggest ways of adapting apparatus. For example, a pupil with a visual impairment might need big numbers on a measuring cylinder in black permanent ink. The TA may also be able to modify and simplify printed material and recording sheets to make them more accessible to individual pupils.

- **Support a pupil**
  For example, if the group is looking at the difference between series and parallel circuits and comparing the effect on three light bulbs, the TA could help set up the experiment and prepare a way for the pupil to record the

Source: © Fox Lane Photography

results – this might be a simple recording format, a photograph or a recording. There are important considerations to be made about this type of support and the way it is delivered so that pupils do not feel stigmatised and different from the rest of the group. It is vital that the TA encourages as much independence as possible for the pupil.

- **Support a group of pupils**
  Imagine that the science teacher has just instructed the whole class to work in groups to find the most acidic household chemical from a range provided; they have to add universal indicator from a dropping bottle and then compare the colours to a pH chart. In a situation such as this, the TA could work within an area of the laboratory, ensuring that pupils have understood what they have to do, checking safety arrangements and improving their understanding of the science involved. Keeping pupils on task, structuring the work and encouraging them to think about what is happening are all valuable parts of a support role.

- **Support the curriculum**
  Consider the situation where a key stage 4 group is planning an experiment to look at osmosis using potatoes. This requires knowledge of cells. If the TA knows the syllabus, the TA can remind the pupils about previous work, making links within the curriculum. Similarly, a TA who has worked with a pupil in other areas of the curriculum can act as a 'bridge' between subjects, emphasising common areas and reminding pupils of, for example, numerical operations learned.

Modifying worksheets

- Use a simple, uncluttered layout and leave a wide margin around the page.
- Use a large font size – 14 pt or larger. Experiment with different styles to find out which is easiest for pupils to read. Pupils with visual impairment will have their preferred font, size and layout on their Education, Health and Care plan.
- Use different colours of paper – pastel shades are often easier to read than black ink on white paper.
- Use subheadings to structure the text and help the reader.
- Break up the text into short chunks or paragraphs; use boxes and bullet points.
- Make use of illustrations if they are helpful to the reader – avoid using them for decoration.
- Separate illustrations/diagrams/tables from the text.
- Avoid double columns of text – make it clear where the reader has to start reading each section.
- Use simple and familiar language. Keep sentences short and concise. Use first person where appropriate for the pupil.
- Highlight and explain key words and any new terminology.

Skills audit

It can be useful for TAs to consider their own strengths and weaknesses within science. (Appendix 5.1 contains a resource that could be used for TA training within science departments to look at their strengths within the subject so they can be deployed to the best advantage within the faculty.) This helps teachers understand how TAs can contribute most effectively to science in the form of knowledge, practical help and behaviour support.

The building of a resource bank of materials to support pupils with SEND is an area where TAs can have a real impact. This activity may involve:

- Sharing ideas and good practice
- Modifying worksheets (under the direction of the teacher)
- Building up a stock of adapted apparatus
- Ensuring effective storage/indexing of resources for future use
- Researching software and internet resources, including apps for tablets

It is important to have a science faculty staff who work together as a team for this to be fully successful, and TAs should be part of this team. The sharing of good practice and a learning philosophy should be paramount in any faculty meetings, and, where possible, TAs should attend.

Observing TAs and offering constructive feedback can be a valuable part of their development. This may be done by the SENCO or faculty staff and may offer opportunities for demonstrating particular skills, for example helping a pupil understand a difficult concept.

It is important to decide on the type of support to be offered and make sure all parties understand the expected outcomes. Will the teacher require support with the whole class? Is it better to support the pupils within a particular group? This can be useful if the groups are organised by attainment. Will certain individual pupils require support, and, if so, is the support best delivered outside the science lab? It is important that these details are discussed with the SEND team and the individual TA. It is also important for TAs to understand what *not* to do and to support pupils in a way that encourages independence rather than dependence (Table 5.1).

Table 5.1 Teaching assistants and pupils with SEND

Avoid. . .	*But instead. . .*
Sitting next to a particular pupil or pupils all the time	Work with other pupils some of the time whilst keeping an eye on the one/ones identified for support
Collecting equipment for the pupil and putting it away (becoming the pupil's 'slave')	Encourage the pupil to do this – with your help if appropriate
Completing a task for the pupil	Ensure that activities are appropriate, and encourage the pupil to work with minimal support
Making decisions for the pupil	Give the pupil opportunities to make choices and decisions – even if you have to limit the options: 'Do you think this. . . or this. . . ?'
Tolerating poor behaviour	Follow the behaviour policy and decide with the teacher on details
Making unnecessary allowances for the pupil	Ensure that pupils follow school rules and take responsibility for their actions
Making unrealistic demands on the pupil	Ensure that instructions are understood and that work is set at an appropriate level
Allowing pupils to become dependent on you	Encourage independence
Confusing the pupil	Make sure you personally understand what is required; be prepared to ask the teacher to repeat something – and be willing to admit not being able to answer a pupil's questions ('I don't know – but let's try to find out' presents a good model of learning behaviour and will win more respect than trying to bluff)

(Continued)

Table 5.1 (Continued)

Avoid. . .	But instead. . .
Using language inappropriate to the pupil	Give short instructions/explanations, and support with visual cues where possible
Trying to become the pupil's 'best friend'	Maintain a friendly but professional relationship
Being indiscreet	Think carefully before sharing information about pupils with staff; the matter of confidentiality should be discussed with the SENCO

Training of teaching assistants

The growth in numbers of TAs and the introduction of higher-level TAs (HLTAs) has spawned a range of training opportunities. Local authorities, academy chains and consortia as well as higher education (HE) providers and commercial organisations offer a wide variety of courses

Talking to the TAs will enable science teachers to gain a greater knowledge of the skills they already have and where there are opportunities for further development.

It is important that the support staff are aware of the ethos behind science teaching. Apart from a knowledge of the actual courses used within the faculty, a basic background of the National Curriculum is very useful.

The National Curriculum for science

The National Curriculum consists of four attainment targets for all key stages. These are:

- Working Scientifically
- Biology
- Chemistry
- Physics

For each key stage there is a programme of study.

The National Curriculum for science aims to ensure that all pupils:

- Develop scientific knowledge and conceptual understanding through the specific disciplines of biology, chemistry and physics

- Develop understanding of the nature, processes and methods of science through different types of science enquiries that help them to answer scientific questions about the world around them
- Are equipped with the scientific knowledge required to understand the uses and implications of science, today and for the future

Additionally, pupils should be able to

- Describe processes and characteristics in common language
- Be familiar with, and use, technical terminology accurately and precisely
- Apply their mathematical knowledge to their understanding of science

Certain skills are required by the TAs, such as the use of questioning to develop the scientific knowledge and confidence of the pupil. The use of questioning is a skill which plays a vital part in the learning of science, and TAs need confidence and training in this. Development of good questioning skills within pupils is also a key skill in developing effective scientists. It is essential to guide all pupils to making sensible choices by using clear language rather than making the choice for them. It is important to know:

- Why are questions asked?
- What are the different types of question?
- How do you ask questions?
- How do you decide on the best question?
- How do you re-frame questions?

The last point needs some further clarity between the TA and teacher, and this is where forward planning is useful because if the TA knows the objectives for the lesson, he or she can re-form the question for the pupil without giving the answer.

It is also important to develop the practical skills of the TAs, and running training sessions for them can enhance their skills. As part of faculty development, training in the use of equipment, especially technology equipment such as tablets, dataloggers and temperature probes, should be a matter of course. It is therefore important to ensure that support staff have a basic scientific knowledge and an understanding of the way to handle equipment. This could be done individually with the TA for your lesson or considered as part of the development of the learning support staff and science faculty staff through work on training days. Appendix 5.2 gives a useful summary sheet for training purposes.

Planning support

Within the science laboratory it is vital that the science teacher and the TA work together. For this to be most effective it is important that TAs:

- Know in advance and understand the objectives, learning outcomes, content of the lesson and any experiments to be undertaken
- Are able to discuss how the work could be differentiated for a particular pupil or group of pupils and know who will make the adjustments to worksheets, etc.
- Along with the teacher, use each other's expertise to develop the skills of the pupil – the TA may have greater understanding of a particular pupil's needs
- Decide prior to the lesson whether the pupil needs time for reinforcement of basic scientific concepts rather than learning a number of new concepts
- Consider whether they will write notes and/or record results for the pupil to enable the pupil to focus on the scientific concepts
- Decide whether the homework will be differentiated by content or outcome
- Know where to sit/stand during the lesson
- Decide how the pupils they support will be grouped within the room

Some of these may seem obvious, but the simplest point can become overlooked and the quality of the support jeopardised.

It is also important that the TA has an adequate scientific knowledge to enable the pupils requiring support to have their learning extended. It is not good enough to have a situation where the TA is learning the scientific skills at the same time as the pupil. If they are to successfully support the pupil they will need to:

- Have a good knowledge of safety rules within the laboratory
- Be confident in handling simple apparatus such as Bunsen burners and measuring cylinders
- Be familiar with where apparatus is stored within the laboratory
- Know how to draw basic tables, charts and graphs
- Be able to manipulate simple scientific equations
- Be able to use ICT equipment such as temperature probes, etc.
- Be familiar with how to complete and record an investigation
- Know where adapted apparatus and worksheets are stored

Medium-term planning is important for any science teacher aiming to be well organised. It enables you to decide if you need to book any specialist equipment or adapt any worksheets or apparatus. It is at this stage that the involvement of support staff can be usefully included. They may be able to suggest practical work that may be more successful for particular pupils or ways of adapting worksheets and differentiating work that will enrich the curriculum for those pupils with special educational needs. Appendix 5.3 gives an example of a planning sheet that can be used.

Short-term planning is important for ordering apparatus and checking work with the support staff. This could be recorded in a diary or kept in a book. Appendix 5.4 has a simple chart for this type of record keeping.

Appendix 5.5 contains an example of a planning sheet that could be used by TAs within science. As a school policy, encouraging TAs to use a diary for recording the type of support they offer and adaptations to work made for pupils could be a valuable record for future referral. At faculty meetings, this information could be shared, and alterations to resources and schemes of work could be made if necessary.

Allow time to discuss the short-term planning with TAs by providing them with the actual plan for a unit of work and asking them for ideas and ways of differentiating aspects of it to suit the pupils they support. This also allows them the opportunity to attend the lessons fully prepared and rightly makes them feel valued.

The support from the TA does not end when the lesson ends. The TA is a valuable source of feedback on how well the pupils met the learning outcomes. This can be used to evaluate the success of the lesson and in particular to evaluate the strategies used with the pupils being supported. Furthermore, it can help determine not only suitable outcomes for the next lesson but also refine how support is used.

Conclusion

- Include the management of TAs in all lesson planning. Be sure about what you want them to do, and be clear about expected outcomes.
- Consider the most effective use of TAs. Can some of their time be spent supporting pupils out of the laboratory or preparing resources?
- Use the TAs' knowledge of particular pupils and their likely difficulties in certain science lessons to pre-empt possible barriers to learning.
- Encourage TAs to access information regarding special adaptations that could be valuable within the laboratory setting.
- Develop the TAs' scientific skills and ensure they have a basic knowledge of science and safety aspects of the subject.
- Include the TAs in the discipline procedure within the laboratory and provide them with training about when it would be appropriate to intervene.

TA support for teachers should enable pupils to:

- Engage and participate in lessons and more social aspects of school
- Become more independent learners
- Achieve and make progress

(Nasen 2014)

6 Real pupils in real classrooms

Eight case studies have been included in this chapter to describe real pupils in science lessons. They may be useful for discussion in departmental training and/or act as a starting point for planning appropriately for similar pupils in your own school.

Individual support plans (previously IEP – Individual Education Plans) may be designed by the SENCO or a member of the learning support team for pupils who are on SEND support or who have an Education, Health and Care plan. Although these are no longer an essential requirement in the 2015 SEND Code of Practice, a majority of schools continue to use these or something similar to be able to closer develop and monitor skills with individual pupils as part of the ongoing assess-plan-do-review cycle. These will often describe generic targets to do with literacy or social skills. It is important that science teachers take note of these targets and incorporate them into their planning. For example, if a pupil's target is to learn to read and spell five new words every week, some of those words could be linked to science. If a target is to 'work independently' for 10 minutes at a time, the science teacher and/or the TA can observe the pupil in science lessons and report back to the SENCO about concentration and task completion. In this way, a coherent approach is achieved, and everyone on the staff is working towards the same goals.

The use of a recording sheet is valuable for liaising with the SENCO about the type and frequency of support that is required for a particular pupil within a science setting. Support plans are also a useful link with the TA who supports the pupil within the science lesson and can link generic targets to specific situations.

The science teacher may be asked to suggest specific science-related targets for support plans or as part of other target-setting systems, and this is an opportunity to be seized upon. Remember that targets need to be SMART (specific, measurable, attainable, relevant and timely): 'to improve in practical work' is too vague, as is 'to work in a group'. Listed in the following are some suggestions which can be adapted for use by the science department. All of these targets can be evidenced by the teacher or TA and kept in a folder to show progress.

Photos can be powerful in providing such evidence; for example, take a photograph of a pupil standing next to her setup experiment and annotate it with details of her achievement using an app such as PicCollage: *'Amandeep collected the apparatus for looking at insulators and conductors. She used the list provided and followed the instructions given to set up the investigation without any help'*. This provides clear evidence of attainment and progress and is highly motivating for pupils (use some for display, in line with school policies).

Individual targets with a science focus

To be able to:

- Collect apparatus for a practical investigation
- Set up apparatus for a practical investigation
- Observe a practical investigation and comment on what has happened
- Record the results from a practical investigation
- Name and spell five/six/ten items of science apparatus
- Say and spell five/ten scientific key words linked to the topic
- Clear away apparatus after a practical investigation
- Set up a practical investigation with a partner, following instructions from the teacher/TA
- Remember and put into action two/three/four instructions
- Stay in seat and 'on task' for 10 minutes without intervention
- Complete homework set for one week and hand it in on time
- Correctly answer a question relating to the practical investigation
- Explain how to test for an acid or alkali, or discuss what seeds need to grow, or explain how to separate mixtures, and demonstrate understanding of what makes a 'fair test'

Case study 1 – Susan, Year 10 (Asperger syndrome)

Susan has an EHC plan and has been diagnosed as having Asperger syndrome. She is a pupil with a mature appearance but immature social skills. She is fairly popular, especially with a group of boys in her class who think she is a laugh. Laura is her best friend; she is protective and will try to stop Susan getting into trouble by doing her work for her. Susan finds it difficult to cope with new situations and can withdraw from group activities. She works best when there are clear instructions and she can work alone or with an able partner. Her language is sophisticated, but the content can be totally irrelevant, and she often has to be brought back to the subject at hand.

Susan has in-class support for English lessons but not for science. Currently she is allowed into lunch for the early sitting as a couple of incidents have occurred recently when she was the focus of some teasing.

How can the science teacher support Susan?

- Break information down into small units of work.
- Label areas where apparatus is stored with pictures/symbols as pupils with Asperger syndrome are often visually perceptive.
- Create a quiet area where Susan can work – she may require greater personal space.
- Introduce only one skill at a time.
- Never demand eye contact.
- Keep your voice calm and allow a certain degree of flexibility.
- Avoid the use of metaphors, idioms and sarcasm.

UNIT: *Control in plants and animals*	LESSON: *1*
Lesson objective (We are learning to. . .)	**Target**
Describe how the parts of the digestive system work together in digestion.	• To work within a small group.
Learning outcomes (What I'm looking for. . .)	**Key words**
ALL pupils should be able to name and locate the organs of the digestive system.	oesophagus, stomach, liver, small intestine, large intestine, peristalsis
MOST pupils should be able to describe the role of these organs.	
SOME pupils should be able to explain how these organs work together in digestion.	

Lesson plan	Apparatus/Resources
Entry activity Word search of different foods and sorting these into groups (revision of food groups). **Starter** Using the torsos, work as a group to place the parts of the digestive system back into place. Time how long it takes; the group with the shortest time wins. **Main** Watch the video about the digestive system. Each group will be given one area of the digestive system that they have to place, describe and explain to the whole class. Provide diagrams of the digestive system for the class to label. **Extension** On diagrams describe what happens to the food at each main point. **Plenary (Assessment)** Ask ten questions about the digestive system. Pupils respond with True/False cards. **Homework** Imagine you are a chip. Describe your passage along the digestive system.	**Adaptations needed for SEN** • No in-class support available for this lesson. • It is important to give Susan a job to do and ensure that she has a part to play when reporting back to the whole group. • Have a writing frame available for the organ given to Susan and her group. • Ensure that Laura is working in a different group. • Susan was told to write what happens to a chip when you eat it, rather than writing it in an imaginary way.

Evaluation of the lesson

Susan initially found it difficult to work within a group even when given a job. She wanted to work in the same group as Laura, and her attention was initially fixed on moving groups. She found the writing frame useful, and this helped her plan the quick presentation. The group gave her a sentence to say within the presentation.

As she found the term 'peristalsis' difficult to understand, next lesson use an orange and a pair of tights to demonstrate this process to give her a concrete way of considering this concept. This will help others within the group who are struggling with this concept.

It was necessary to take a couple of minutes after the lesson to explain the homework to Susan and tell her she only had to say what happened in each part of the digestive system.

Case study 2 – Ashraf, Year 8 (cerebral palsy)

Ashraf has cerebral palsy and learning difficulties and has an EHC plan. He uses a wheelchair to move between lessons and a K-walker for moving around the classroom. He can speak but is very reluctant to do so in class. Ashraf has a laptop computer that he uses for all writing tasks. He is working at level P7 in Science and below age-related expectations in English.

Ashraf has a one-to-one teaching assistant because of his learning and personal needs. She and the science teacher planned the unit of work together to ensure that there were activities within each lesson that would be appropriate and that would support his individual targets. The teaching assistant has prepared a specific writing frame for Ashraf to record results. The teacher has asked the teaching assistant to support Ashraf within a small group rather than on his own. This group will vary according to the nature of the activity.

How can the science teacher support Ashraf?

- Check Ashraf's support plan frequently to see current targets.
- Breaking the work into small units will be valuable.
- Consider the layout of the room for wheelchair and walking-aid access.
- Allow plenty of time for answering questions.
- Adapt apparatus as necessary.
- Liaise with the TA before lessons so she understands the work to be covered and the learning objectives for Ashraf.

UNIT: Compounds and mixtures | *LESSON: 2*

Lesson objective (We are learning to. . .)

Use the idea of changes in reactions to describe these as either chemical or physical reactions. *(Ashraf is working at level P7: Pupils understand the scientific use of some simple vocabulary, such as before, after, bumpy, grow, eat, and move and can communicate related ideas and observations using simple phrases. They make simple records of their findings [for example, by putting pictures of an activity in sequence]. They begin to make suggestions for planning and evaluating their work [for example, responding to the question 'Was that right or wrong?']. 'Showing', 'demonstrating' 'trying out' 'responding' etc. may be done by any means appropriate to the pupil's preferred mode of communication and physical abilities.)*

Support plan targets

- Complete a simple task without help.
- Use symbols identifying the key words (colour change and temperature change) in the correct context.

(Continued)

UNIT: Compounds and mixtures	*LESSON: 2*

Learning outcomes (What I'm looking for. . .)	**Key words**
ALL should be able to recognise changes in colour and temperature in reactions.	colour change, chemical change, chemical reaction, physical reaction, compound, mixture
MOST should be able to classify these changes as reversible or non-reversible.	
SOME will be able to use this to define chemical and physical reactions.	

Lesson plan	*Apparatus/Resources*
Entry activity Sorting cards into elements and compounds.	**Adaptations needed for SEN**
Starter Ask 10 questions, which pupils answer with Yes/No cards, on everyday reactions and whether these are reversible, e.g., fry an egg, boil a kettle of water.	• Adapted Bunsen burner and test tubes heated in a retort stand for extra stability.
Main Carry out test tube reactions where visible changes take place, such as adding lead nitrate to potassium iodide, dilute hydrochloric acid to magnesium carbonate powder, heating sugar, melting ice, dissolving salt, and adding dilute ammonia solution to copper sulphate solution. Record observations.	• Ashraf is working with two other pupils. He has to tell the TA how to set up heating sugar and then has to adjust the Bunsen burner. • A worksheet is available with a table drawn on it for the results, which has been put onto his laptop.
Extension Describe how you could reverse any of the prior reactions.	
Plenary (Assessment) In groups agree on a short paragraph about whether the reactions were reversible or not, giving evidence. Then look at the paragraph of another group, see if you agree and give them feedback.	
Homework	

Evaluation of the lesson

Ashraf found it difficult to pick up the cards and identify elements and compounds; maybe next time he could practise the key vocabulary terms with his TA while other pupils complete this task. Working in a group, he found it difficult to express his ideas but was able to explain them to the TA. He told the other group during the plenary session that the reaction between lead nitrate and potassium iodide showed a 'colour change', and, after questioning, he told the TA that ice melting had a 'change of temperature'. Ashraf worked well and showed he remembered where the basic apparatus was kept. He was able to light the Bunsen burner himself, changing it to a blue flame.

Case study 3 – Jenny, Year 7 (Down syndrome)

Jenny has Down syndrome and has an EHC plan. She is a very confident pupil who has a lot of support from home. She is assertive, and this can lead to her being obstinate. Generally she is working below age-related expectations in most subjects. She has worked with a teaching assistant on safety around school and how to behave in practical subjects, and this is regularly reinforced as she has a social story written about her behaviour in practical subjects in her diary. She reads through this with her TA in school and with her mother at home.

She has started to put on weight and tries to avoid PE; her mother will write her notes so she can avoid physical activities.

Although she was happy at primary school, she is beginning to notice she is different from the older girls, and her friends from her previous school have made other friends and she feels excluded.

Jenny is in set 4 for science. This is a small group of 15 pupils, and there are two TAs present. She needs reminding frequently about safety points, such as wearing goggles, and she needs to be made to follow basic classroom rules. She has a 'buddy' for this academic year in science. Gemma volunteered to be Jenny's partner as she likes her and enjoys the responsibility of working with her. Jenny looks up to Gemma and is very keen to do as she says. The teacher and the two TAs work together to plan the science lessons and gather resources for the entire class. Both TAs are confident working with Jenny, and she knows and respects them both. She finds aspects of chemistry and physics difficult.

How can the science teacher support Jenny?

- Provide opportunities for plenty of reinforcement of basic knowledge and skills.
- Give her help with handling apparatus. She often does not know when something is full, so provide a probe with buzzer.
- Adapted worksheets will be required.
- Consider different ways of recording results – using pictures or symbols can be very helpful, as well as pre-prepared results tables and a writing frame.
- Introduce new vocabulary gradually and explain carefully.
- Praise Jenny for her efforts – and remember to acknowledge the work of her buddy.
- Liaise with TAs on a regular basis, and make sure they understand the lesson objectives.

UNIT: *Acids and alkalis*   LESSON: *3*

Lesson objective (We are learning to. . .)

Use indicators to test different solutions to find out how acidic or alkaline they are.

Learning outcomes (What I'm looking for. . .)

ALL should be able to describe how universal indicator gives a range of colours with acids and alkalis.

MOST should be able to classify solutions as acids and alkalis using the pH scale.

SOME will be able to relate the strength of an acid or alkali to its pH.

Support plan targets

- Follow simple instructions.
- Use scientific words correctly.

Key words

acid, alkali, neutral, pH metre, pH paper, universal indicator

---

Lesson plan

Entry activity
Matching hazard symbols to descriptions.

Starter
Ask them to hold up the right card in response to 10 starter questions.

Set of three cards, each a different colour: red = acid, green = neutral, purple = alkali.

Main
Explain idea of weak and strong acids and alkalis. Show them how to test the pH with a colour card and check with a pH metre. On pH scale in exercise books, write the words 'weak acid', 'strong acid', 'weak alkali', and 'strong alkali', giving corresponding numbers.

Test a range of solutions with universal indicator and record the findings in a table.

Extension
Write the name of the solution onto their pH scales.

Plenary (Assessment)
pH maths: give each pupil a set of cards the same colours as the pH scale. Hold up cards at the front to illustrate a sum, e.g., purple (pH 12) subtract yellow (pH 6) equals? The pupils respond with their cards, e.g., yellow (pH 6).

Homework
Test household chemicals using universal indicator paper.

Apparatus/Resources

Adaptations needed for SEN

- A worksheet will be needed for Jenny with a table drawn out for her to fill in the colour; she will use coloured crayons rather than writing. She will be able to write the pH numbers.
- pH scale as worksheet with words: strong acid, weak acid, neutral, strong alkali, weak alkali. Jenny is expected to put arrows to the correct place on the scale from these words.
- Jenny can work with Gemma, her buddy, with a TA supporting a small group of boys in same area.

Evaluation of the lesson

Jenny was able to collect apparatus and handle test tubes. She initially spilt some liquids whilst pouring because she did not stop pouring quickly enough when the buzzer sounded, and she forgot to use the buzzer on another occasion. Next time the group has to pour from bottles, TA support will be needed. Jenny asked Gemma what to do with the worksheet; because Gemma was working in her book, Jenny started to copy her. The worksheet where she had to match key words worked well and allowed her to make a suggestion during the plenary activity. As the practical work was broken down into smaller units of work, she coped well.

Case study 4 – Steven, Year 8 (social, emotional and mental health needs)

Steven had significant social and emotional problems in primary school and came to the secondary school on the SEND support register. He had a number of exclusions because of his behaviour towards pupils and staff; currently, the school is waiting to see if his application for an EHC plan will be accepted. He was placed on Ritalin during the summer holiday (prescribed to help manage symptoms of ADHD), and since he returned in September there has been a significant improvement in his behaviour. Steven is working at age-related expectations. He is not well-liked by other pupils as he tends to bully them and steal things, such as a shoe, to annoy others. Since his mother started a new relationship he has been excluded for throwing a chair and has been cautioned by the police for stealing from a local DIY store.

In Year 8 the groups are streamed, and it was decided to put Steven in the bottom set where there is support. A TA works with a small group, but when Steven has difficulties the TA has to withdraw him from the lesson.

How can the science teacher support Steven?

- Keep instructions short and clear, giving enough processing time for Steven to be able to respond. If repetition is needed, repeat them in the same tone of voice.
- When talking with him, ensure he is paying attention.
- Break the lesson into small units.
- Use praise but make it very specific – use rewards like certificates.
- Keep calm when dealing with him as he will mirror you.
- Have clear laboratory routines and give him something responsible to do so other pupils see him in a positive light.
- Give advance warning of any changes.
- When offering choices, give him no more than two.
- Worksheets need to be clearly presented and free from unnecessary information or pictures.
- Give him some responsibility, e.g., handing out worksheets.

UNIT: Food and digestion	LESSON: 4

Lesson objective (We are learning to. . .)

Describe how the size of the food particles is important for absorption.

Support plan targets

- To complete the written work set for the lesson.
- Put up hand when answering questions.

Learning outcomes (What I'm looking for. . .)

ALL should be able to describe that starch, protein and fat molecules are too big to be absorbed.

MOST should explain how these larger particles can be broken down into smaller ones.

SOME will be able to explain this using the idea of the sizes of hole in the wall of the small intestines.

Key words

digestion, molecule, starch, sugar, small intestine

Lesson plan	*Apparatus/Resources*

Entry activity
Place pictures of different foods into groups to show which of the food groups they are rich in.

Starter
Split the class into four groups with a model torso or large diagram each. Question and answer session: if a member of the group gets a question right, they place a digestive organ on the torso/diagram. The winning group is the first one with a complete digestive system.

Main
Start by sorting large and small building blocks through holes; use the results of this to predict whether large starch molecules will be able to pass through the wall of the intestines.

Class practical with starch and glucose solution inside Visking tubing, placed in a beaker of water.

Test the water from the beaker for starch and glucose every 5 minutes for 20 minutes.

Write an explanation of their findings, again using the building blocks as a model to help with this.

Adaptations needed for SEN

- This lesson contains many opportunities for Steven to take turns. The writing is also broken up into smaller units to enable him and others in the group to cope with the written work expected.
- Before Steven begins his practical work, he has to write a risk assessment of the lesson and have it checked.
- Steven is encouraged to use key words on cards as a method of organising his thoughts. The TA is present but working with another group of pupils who need support with the practical work.

Lesson plan	*Apparatus/Resources*

Plenary (Assessment)
Provide information cards on proteins and amino acids; use these to explain which will pass through the wall of the intestines. Discuss in groups and report back to the rest of the class.

Homework

Evaluation of the lesson

It would have been useful to have a worksheet with practical instructions for Steven as he found it difficult to remember all the details. He needed four reminders to put his hand up during the lesson. He did not have to leave the room owing to poor behaviour in this lesson.

Case study 5 – Lucy, Year 10 (dyspraxia)

Lucy has an EHC plan because of her dyspraxia. She has very supportive parents who still use a home/school book. Lucy has found making friends difficult and spends break and most lunchtimes in the learning resources area. She was bullied in Year 8 by a small group of challenging girls, but in some ways this gave her credibility with her peers, and she felt accepted because of the bullying. She is following GCSE courses and is predicted to get grades 5/6 in most subjects. She can now find her way around school but needs help with following her Year 10 timetable. A TA goes through it with her each morning before the start of school. It is best to place Lucy in a group that matches her ability level, but this can be difficult to judge.

Lucy has 10 hours of support as a result of her EHC plan, but this is not always available for science lessons. When completing practice and timed exams, Lucy will require support to help her sort out her work and develop her thought sequencing. Writing frames support her and are an aid to develop her thinking skills. Lucy does not like new situations and suffers from panic attacks.

How can the science teacher support Lucy?

- Be sensitive to Lucy's limitations in practical work, and plan tasks carefully to enable success.
- Liaise with the TA and ask her to prepare Lucy for practical sessions beforehand by going through the method and helping her organise her thoughts.
- Consider the use of adapted equipment, and use a shallow-sided tray for carrying out practical work. Provide a plastic apron to avoid injury with chemicals.
- Check Lucy's understanding of instructions/tasks.
- Structure written work by using writing frames.
- Take extra care with safety issues.

UNIT: Chemical reactions   *LESSON: 5*

Lesson objective (We are learning to. . .)   **Support plan target**

Plan and make predictions about what affects the rate of the reaction between sodium thiosulphate and hydrochloric acid.

- Sequence simple instructions.

UNIT: *Chemical reactions*	LESSON: *5*

Learning outcomes (What I'm looking for. . .)

ALL should be able to describe how to measure the rate of reaction.

MOST should plan a fair test by controlling variables.

SOME should make predictions based on understanding of particles.

Key words

rate of reaction, measuring cylinder, concentration, temperature, conical flask

Lesson plan	*Apparatus/Resources*

Entry activity
Concept cartoon where the pupils have to decide which statement about rates of reaction is correct and why.

Adaptations needed for SEN

- Use a computer simulation to show Lucy that reactions take place at different speeds. She will be able to change the particle size in this simulation.
- Lucy could use different sizes of jelly particles dissolving in water if the sodium thiosulphate and hydrochloric acid investigation proves too difficult.
- The TA is not available for this lesson but could support the homework over a lunchtime.

Starter
Demo the chemical reaction between sodium thiosulphate and hydrochloric acid. Each group has to try to write the word equation for this reaction by rearranging cards containing the names of the molecules.

Main
Use the investigation planning posters (A4 size) to plan a fair test into what would affect the rate of this reaction. This should be individual work.

Time should be spent on the prediction using a supplementary exercise to remind pupils about particle size and speed.

(Continued)

Lesson plan	*Apparatus/Resources*

Plenary (Assessment)

Give out plans for other investigations; in groups the pupils have to spot the errors in these plans and explain what needs to be done to put them right.

Homework

Ensure plans are complete and ready to start practical work next lesson.

Evaluation of the lesson

During the previous lesson, Lucy was told that today we would be performing part of a piece of GCSE coursework so that she was more prepared and would not panic. She was still concerned when she came in, but using the computer and previously talking with her helper to reassure her of her ability to complete the task had calmed her down. Using jelly rather than sodium thiosulphate gave her a better base for her prediction because she was used to making jelly at home. She found the investigation planning sheet useful to scaffold her writing and sequence her ideas.

Case study 6 – Megan, Year 10 (spina bifida)

Megan is very outgoing, loud and tough. She has spina bifida and uses a wheelchair. She has an EHC plan which specifies support for her personal care as well as educational support. She has her own laptop computer which she uses for all recording in lessons. Megan has a very forthright personality and has upset some of the TAs with her brusque manner. Recently she turned her wheelchair around so that her back was facing the supply teacher, and she has made cutting remarks to a very sensitive girl in the same class. She has recently failed to complete homework. Megan works hard when she likes a subject and is expected to get grades 2–4 in her GCSEs and to do especially well in mathematics and science.

How can the science teacher support Megan?

- Ensure free access around the lab for Megan's wheelchair. Keep bags and coats off the floor.
- Sit down to talk with Megan when possible – rather than looking down over her all the time.
- Have high expectations.
- Liaise with the TA about the strategy for each lesson – consider whether it is best to ask the TA to write the results or to do the experiment sometimes to avoid Megan becoming too tired.
- Have a range of adapted apparatus and use a very shallow-sided tray for carrying out practical work. Provide a plastic apron to avoid injury with chemicals.
- Allow Megan to leave the lesson ahead of other pupils to give her plenty of time to get to the next lesson.

UNIT: *Waves in action*	LESSON: 6
Lesson objective (We are learning to. . .)	**Support plan target**
Describe how total internal reflection is used in a range of devices.	• Complete all work set including homework.
Learning outcomes (What I'm looking for. . .)	**Key words**
ALL will be able to draw and interpret simple ray diagrams.	ray, normal, total internal reflection, periscope, endoscope
MOST will be able to explain that total internal reflection occurs at angles greater than the critical angle.	
SOME will be able to explain how total internal reflection is used in various optical devices.	

Lesson plan	Apparatus/Resources
Entry activity Label a diagram to revise the key words when investigating reflection of light waves.	**Adaptations needed for SEN** • Care required, as at some parts of the lesson the room needs to be darkened; this could cause problems with wheelchair movement.
Starter Draw and explain to a partner the main parts of a wave, then write a mnemonic for the different parts of the wave.	• It is important to make sure that Megan's group has apparatus set up before the lights go out. The apparatus needs to be set up on the lower table. A TA is available this lesson, but she will not be with Megan unless she needs help.
Main Collect light apparatus and set up an investigation into how the passage of light through a semi-circular Perspex block is affected by different angles. Draw results, putting the normal line on diagrams. Teacher explanation of total internal reflection. Use the worksheet to explain how periscopes, endoscopes and optical fibres work.	• There is a computer simulation for Megan to use if she chooses. • Her homework diary needs to be checked by the teacher to ensure that she has recorded her homework.
Plenary (Assessment) Provide a series of diagrams showing light entering different-shaped Perspex blocks at different angles; the pupils need to use their knowledge of total internal reflection and refraction to draw where these rays would then go.	
Homework On diagrams of a periscope and an endoscope, draw the ray diagrams and explain how these work.	

Evaluation of the lesson

Megan found it difficult to place the Perspex block in exactly the right place but did not want to use the computer simulation. The TA had to remind her about her homework the next day because she had not completed it. There were some problems with the movement of the wheelchair after the lights went out as Megan insisted on moving to talk to a friend.

Case study 7 – Harry, Year 7 (dyslexia)

Harry is dyslexic and is on the SEND support stage of intervention. He was very anxious about his transfer to secondary school in September, even though he made two extra visits to try to alleviate his anxieties. Harry really enjoys music and has joined the school choir, which has helped him make friends with some of the boys. He finds it difficult to tell left from right and has poor short-term memory. He achieves well in verbal presentations, but literacy skills and personal organisation are poor.

Harry has one-to-one support in English and is working towards age-related expectations. He is withdrawn for small-group work on literacy skills and is part of a paired reading scheme two mornings a week before school.

How can the science teacher support Harry?

- Look for strengths within science and work from this base.
- Give plenty of praise.
- Make the work visual with a lot of picture and flow charts.
- Encourage the use of ICT and spell-checkers to develop self-esteem.
- Provide a list of key words.
- Use writing frames and experiment with coloured overlays to help with reading. Try printing worksheets on pastel-coloured paper.
- Allow adequate time to finish work.
- Use differentiated worksheets, using cloze procedure and pictures.
- Ensure different strategies are offered to the whole class rather than singling out Harry for special attention.

UNIT: Energy resources   *LESSON: 7*

Lesson objective (We are learning to. . .)	**Support plan targets**
Describe the various sources of energy available to us.	<ul><li>Write four sentences using a list of key words.</li><li>Remember to bring equipment to the lesson.</li></ul>

Learning outcomes (What I'm looking for. . .)	**Key words**
ALL must use the names for the main renewable and non-renewable energy sources accurately. **MOST** will be able to describe the difference between renewable and non-renewable energy sources. **SOME** will be able to use the idea 'sustainable' energy sources.	energy, force, power, fuel, fossil fuel, non-renewable and renewable energy resources

---

Lesson plan	Apparatus/Resources
Entry activity Word search with the names of different energy sources; they need to sort these into renewable and non-renewable.	**Adaptations needed for SEN** • Have examples of fossil fuels and pictures of renewable energy sources available for any pupil to use.
Starter Selected pupils will present their designs for a low-energy usage device powered by renewable energy sources (last lesson's homework) to the rest of the class.	• Sit Harry next to someone who reads well but is not overpowering; he could 'share notes' with them if necessary.
Main Pupils work individually on poster paper to produce a poster or concept map or spider diagram to describe the energy sources available. Within this they should distinguish between renewable and non-renewable sources.	• Have an example of a concept map and spider diagram to show the class before they begin the activity. • No TA works with Harry in science.
Extension Wood can be described as both renewable and non-renewable – how can this be?	
Plenary (Assessment) Pupils swap posters and mark these against the given criteria and report back to the group which produced the poster.	
Homework Find out what energy sources you use at home.	

Evaluation of the lesson

Harry had completed his homework but made a model of his device rather than write about it, so he was asked to share it with the rest of the class. At the end of the lesson a photo of it was taken and stuck in Harry's book. He found it difficult to keep on task initially, but being able to have examples of fuels in front of him helped, as well as being able to use pictures to stick on his work. As others were also using computers for their written work, he felt quite happy writing six sentences to stick on his poster. Initially he was negative about his poster, but when marked against the criteria it received positive comments from others. His partner did most of the written work, but Harry did supply a lot of the ideas. Next time it would be useful for him to plan his ideas on paper so he has to do some of the writing.

Case study 8 – Bhavini, Year 9 (visual impairment)

Bhavini has an EHC plan as she has very limited vision and uses a stick around school. Some pupils have made hurtful comments to her about this. To enhance her sight she has to wear very thick lens glasses, which she hates. She often recognises people by their voices. Outside school she is an active member of the Phab Club (a club for physically handicapped as well as able-bodied teenagers). She goes on outings with them and plays sport but does not like sport in school.

Bhavini has in-class support but wants to be independent around school and so refuses help at the change-over of lessons. The key TA will enlarge work for her and photocopy work to rearrange it in a more visually friendly way; sometimes she will record information and homework instructions onto tape. Bhavini has her own personal voice recorder with headphones. She always carries a bubble magnifier and has access to a CCTV. She can read Braille.

How can the science teacher support Bhavini?

- Allow her to sit sideways to the teacher so that she can easily hear both the teacher and the rest of the group.
- Ensure lighting is good.
- Avoid standing with your back to the window; this makes it harder for Bhavini to see you.
- If using a textbook, ensure that Bhavini has one of her own, if it has not been possible to modify the appropriate pages in advance. The Local Authority Sensory Support Service should have an enlarged copy of the textbook that they can lend the school.
- Be aware that she may tire easily.
- Use adapted equipment such as talking scales, and have a thermistor attached to a buzzer for measuring when containers are full. (The LA VI service will be able to help out with this. The Royal National Institute for the Blind [RNIB] is also a useful source of information.)
- Label apparatus stores in Braille as well as words.
- Use descriptive language.
- Ensure the CCTV is accessible, either by having it brought to the classroom (they are heavy and bulky to move) or by arranging for Bhavini to access it with another member of staff.

UNIT: Energy and electricity	*LESSON: 8*

Lesson objective (We are learning to. . .)

Describe how electricity is generated.

Learning outcomes (What I'm looking for. . .)

ALL should be able to describe how electricity can be made by a motion between a coil and a magnet.

MOST should be able to explain how this movement can be caused by burning a fossil fuel.

SOME will be able to describe the implications of the fact that electricity can't be stored easily.

Support plan target

- To make greater use of the magnifier.

Key words

electricity, generator, power station

Lesson plan	*Apparatus/Resources*

Entry activity
Crossword based on fossil fuels.

Starter
Ask them to work in groups, and in five sentences explain where electricity comes from to power a computer. Draw together some of the answers and write these on the board.

Main
Demonstrate a bicycle dynamo. Show that as more energy is provided, there is a greater output. Show a video about generating electricity in power stations which use a range of different fuels.

Draw flow diagrams to show how the energy stored in the fuel is transferred to leave ultimately as electricity.

In groups, use kits to make a generator which will light a light bulb and describe how these work.

Extension
Research how pumped-storage power stations are used to provide electricity at peak times.

Adaptations needed for SEN

- Bhavini's group should record their sentences on a voice recorder as well as writing them on paper, but Bhavini should be asked to read one sentence the group has recorded. The blinds will need to be closed so that Bhavini can see the light on the dynamo.
- Have an enlarged worksheet to be used with the magnifier (if necessary) for her with the key ideas from the video. She is to circle the key points as she hears them; this will require planning before the lesson.
- Bhavini's group should make their generator sound a buzzer rather than light a bulb.

Lesson plan	*Apparatus/Resources*

Plenary (Assessment)

Use mini whiteboards to answer a series of questions based on the energy transfer at various stages in the process of the generation of electricity.

Homework

Evaluation of the lesson

Bhavini was able to read out a sentence using the magnifier, but she found it difficult to see the light on the dynamo, although she heard the buzzer with her group's generator. Others enjoyed taping their ideas, and it was easy for her to become more involved with the group for this section of the lesson. The worksheet worked well and needs to be stored for future use.

Resources and useful websites

ASE resources: www.ase.org.uk/resources/send/

Crick Software (Clicker, Find Out and Write About):
Crick House
Boarden Close
Moulton Park
Northampton NN3 6LF
Tel: 01604 671 691, fax: 01604 671 692
email: info@cricksoft.com, website: www.cricksoft.com

Rob Butler provides up-to-date information, resources and teaching tips for science: https://fiendishlyclever.com

Concept Cartoons:
Millgate House Publishing
Unit 1, Wheelock Heath Business Court,
Alsager Road,
Winterley,
Sandbach. CW11 4RQ
Email: keepintouch@millgatehouse.co.uk, website: www.millgatehouse.co.uk

General advice for SEN and inclusion:
https://senexchangeuk.wordpress.com/

NRS Healthcare (products for occupational therapy and rehabilitation):
Telephone: 0354 121 8111, fax: 0845 121 8112
www.nrshealthcare.co.uk

STEM Learning – SEN in the science department:
www.stem.org.uk/elibrary/collection/2985/sen-in-the-science-department

Times Educational Supplement Website for free resources such as images of equipment to post on the walls, pupil record sheets and sentence starters:

www.tes.com/teaching-resource/science-equipment-diagrams-for-wall-display-6090129

Widget (communicate in print symbols, Symwriter):
www.widgit.com

Winscope – to digitise any waveform:
www.zelscope.com

All details correct May 2016.

Appendix 1.1   Legislation and guidance

The Children and Families Act: a different landscape

The Children and Families Act 2014 introduced radical changes to the requirements placed on both schools and teachers regarding the education and inclusion of pupils with special educational needs and disabilities. The first major revision of the SEN framework for 30 years, it introduced a new system to help children with special educational needs and disabilities and shaped how education, health and social care professionals should work in partnership with children, young people and their families.

The reforms introduced a system to support children and young people from birth up to the age of 25 in a way that is designed to ensure smooth transitions across all services as they move from school into further education, training and employment. The reforms give particular emphasis to preparing children and young people for adulthood from the earliest years. This means enabling children to be involved at as young an age as possible in all decisions relating to their learning, therapy, medical treatment and support from social care. The result of this preparation should be that when young people reach the age of 16, they are able to be full and active participants in all important decisions about their life.

There is now an important distinction made between a child and a young person. The Act gives significant new rights directly to young people when they are over compulsory school age but under the age of 25. Under the Act, a child becomes a young person after the last day of summer term during the academic year in which he or she turns 16. This is subject to a young person 'having capacity' to take a decision under the Mental Capacity Act 2005.

Throughout this book the term 'pupils with special educational needs and disabilities (SEND)' is used. A pupil has special educational needs if he or she:

- Has a significantly greater difficulty in learning than the majority of others of the same age or
- Has a disability which prevents or hinders him or her from making use of facilities of a kind generally provided for others of the same age in mainstream schools or mainstream Post-16 institutions (SEND Code of Practice 2015)

Section 19 principles

Central to Part 3 of the Children and Families Act 2014 is Section 19. This section emphasises the role to be played by parents/carers and young people themselves in all decision making about their SEND provision.

Part C of Section 19 issues a new challenge to schools in that there is a clear expectation that parents and pupils will not only be invited to participate but that they should be supported to do so. This will certainly involve the provision of relevant information to parents, but schools could also consider providing other forms of support – both practical support, such as helping with translation services or even transport to attend important meetings, and emotional support, such as advocacy or pre-meetings to prepare parents and pupils to take a full part in all decisions. Many parents will need only a minimal level of additional support, but others – especially those often portrayed as 'hard to reach' – may require considerably more.

Key questions

- Do you know the wishes and feelings about education of your pupils with SEND and their parents? If not, how can you find out?
- What could you and others in your subject/departmental team do to integrate this information into your planning for and delivery of teaching and learning?
- What more could you do to reach out to parents who may be anxious about or unwilling to engage with school?

The SEND Code of Practice

SEND provision is provision that is additional to or different from the high quality, differentiated teaching to which all pupils are entitled. A school's first response to a pupil falling behind his or her peers should be to evaluate the quality of teaching and learning the pupil currently receives in all subjects. The pupil should be identified as having SEND only when the school is confident that all teaching is differentiated appropriately to meet that individual pupil's needs.

Once a pupil is identified as having SEND, schools are required to do whatever they can to remove any barriers to learning and to put in place effective provision, or 'SEND Support'. This support must enable pupils with SEND to achieve the best possible outcomes.

Most schools and academies welcome pupils with a range of vulnerabilities, including special educational needs and disabilities, but may hesitate about including those with significant or complex needs. The reasons behind this reluctance are often a lack of expertise in an area of need, worries about behaviour and, most commonly expressed, concerns about the impact of that pupil's needs on the education of others.

The SEND Code of Practice is very clear that where the parent of a pupil with an Education, Health, and Care plan (EHC plan) makes a request for a particular school, the local authority **must** comply with that preference and name the school in the plan unless:

- it would be unsuitable for the age, ability, aptitude or SEN of the child or young person, or
- the attendance of the child or young person there would be incompatible with the efficient education of others, or the efficient use of resources.

(SEND Code of Practice 2015, 9.79, p. 172)

Legally, schools cannot refuse to admit a pupil who does not have an EHC plan because they do not feel able to cater for his or her needs or because the pupil does not have an EHC plan.

Outcomes

Outcomes are written from the perspective of the pupil and should identify what the provision is intended to achieve. For example, do you think the following is an outcome for a pupil in Year 7 with literacy difficulties?

'For the next 10 weeks Jake will work on an online literacy programme for 20 minutes three times each week'.

It may be specific and measurable; it is achievable and realistic; and it is time targeted, so it is 'SMART', but it isn't an 'outcome'. What is described here is provision – i.e., the intervention the school will use to help Jake make accelerated progress.

Outcomes are intended to look forward to the end of the next stage or phase of education, usually two or three years hence. Teachers will, of course, set short-term targets covering between 6 and 12 weeks and EHC plans will also include interim objectives to be discussed at annual reviews. So what would be an outcome for Jake?

'By the end of Year 9, Jake will be able to read and understand the textbooks for his chosen GCSE courses'.

The online literacy course would then form a part of the package of provision to enable Jake to achieve this outcome.

The graduated approach

The 2015 SEND Code of Practice describes SEND support as a cyclical process of assess, plan, do and review that is known as the 'graduated approach'. This cycle is already commonly used in schools, and for pupils with SEND it is intended to be much more than a token, in-house process. Rather it should be a powerful mechanism for reflection and evaluation of the impact of SEND provision. Through the four-part cycle, decisions and actions are revisited, refined and revised. This then leads to a deeper understanding of an individual pupil's needs whilst also offering insight into the effectiveness of the school's overall provision for pupils with SEND. The graduated approach offers the school, the pupil and his or her parents a growing understanding of the needs of the pupil and what provision the pupil requires to enable him or her to make good progress and secure good outcomes. Through successive cycles, the graduated approach draws on increasingly specialist expertise, assessments and approaches and more frequent reviews. This structured process gives teachers the information they need to match specific, evidenced-based interventions to pupils' individual needs.

Evidenced-based interventions

In recent years, a number of universities and other research organisations have produced evidence about the efficacy of a range of different interventions for vulnerable pupils and pupils with SEND. Most notable among this research is that sponsored by the *Education Endowment Fund* that offers schools valid data on the impact of interventions and the optimal conditions for their use. Other important sources of information about evidence-based interventions for specific areas of need are the *Communication Trust 'What Works?'* website and *'Interventions for Literacy'* from the *SpLD/Dyslexia Trust*. Both sites offer transparent and clear information for professionals and parents to support joint decisions about provision.

The Equality Act 2010

Sitting alongside the Children and Families Act 2014, the requirements of the Equality Act 2010 remain firmly in place. This is especially important because many children and young people who have SEND may also have a disability under the Equality Act. The definition of disability in the Equality Act is that the child or young person has ' . . . a physical or mental impairment which has a long-term and substantial adverse effect on a person's ability to carry out normal day-to-day activities'.

'Long-term' is defined as lasting or being likely to last for 'a year or more', and 'substantial' is defined as 'more than minor or trivial'. The definition includes sensory impairments such as those affecting sight or hearing and, just as crucially for schools, children with long-term health conditions such as asthma, diabetes, epilepsy and cancer.

As the SEND Code of Practice (DfE 2015: 16) states, the definition for disability provides a relatively low threshold and includes many more children than schools may realise. Children and young people with some conditions do not necessarily have SEND, but there is often a significant overlap between disabled children and young people and those with SEND. Where a disabled child or young person requires special educational provision, they also will be covered by the SEND duties.

The Equality Act applies to all schools including academies and free schools, University Technical Colleges and Studio Schools, as well as further education colleges and sixth form colleges – even where the school or college has no disabled pupils currently on roll. This is because the duties under the Equality Act are anticipatory in that they cover not only current pupils but also prospective ones. The expectation is that all schools will be reviewing accessibility continually and making reasonable adjustments in order to improve access for disabled pupils. When thinking about disabled access, the first thing school leaders usually consider is physical access, such as wheelchair access, lifts and ramps. But physical access is only part of the requirement of the Equality Act and often is the simplest to improve. Your school's accessibility plan for disabled pupils must address all three elements of planned improvements in access:

1   Physical improvements to increase access to education and associated services
2   Improvements in access to the curriculum
3   Improvements in the provision of information for disabled pupils in a range of formats

Improvements in access to the curriculum are often a harder nut to crack as they involve all departments and all teachers looking closely at their teaching and learning strategies and evaluating how effectively these meet the needs of disabled pupils. Often, relatively minor amendments to the curriculum or teaching approaches can lead to major improvements in access for disabled pupils, and these often have a positive impact on the education of all pupils. For example, one school installed a Soundfield amplification system in a number of classrooms because a pupil with hearing loss had joined the school. The following year, the cohort of Year 7 pupils had particularly poor speaking and listening skills, and it was noticed that they were more engaged in learning when they were taught in the rooms with the Soundfield system. This led to improvements in progress for the whole cohort and significantly reduced the level of disruption and off-task behaviours in those classes.

Schools also have wider duties under the Equality Act to prevent discrimination, to promote equality of opportunity and to foster good relations. These duties should inform all aspects of school improvement planning from curriculum design through to anti-bullying policies and practice.

Significantly, a pupil's underachievement or behaviour difficulties might relate to an underlying physical or mental impairment which could be covered by the Equality Act. Each pupil is different and will respond to situations in his or her unique way so a disability should be considered in the context of the child as an individual. The 'social model' of disability sees the environment as the primary disabling factor, as opposed to the 'medical model' that focuses on the individual child's needs and difficulties. School activities and environments should be considered in the light of possible barriers to learning or participation.

Appendix 1.2   Departmental policy

Whether the practice in your school is to have separate SEND policies for each department or to embed the information on SEND in your whole-school Inclusion or Teaching and Learning policies, the processes and information detailed here will still be relevant.

Good practice for pupils with SEND and disabilities is good practice for all pupils, especially those who are 'vulnerable' to underachievement. Vulnerable groups may include looked-after children (LAC), pupils for whom English is an additional language (EAL), pupils from minority ethnic groups, young carers and pupils known to be eligible for free school meals/ Pupil Premium funding. Be especially aware of those pupils with SEND who face one or more additional vulnerabilities and for whom effective support might need to go beyond help in the classroom.

It is crucial that your departmental or faculty policy describes a strategy for meeting pupils' special educational needs within your particular curricular area. The policy should set the scene for any visitor, from supply staff to inspectors, and make a valuable contribution to the departmental handbook. The process of developing a department SEND policy offers the opportunity to clarify and evaluate current thinking and practice within the Science team and to establish a consistent approach.

The SEND policy for your department is a significant document in terms of the leadership and management of your subject. The preparation and review of the policy should be led by a senior manager within the team because that person needs to have sufficient status to be able to influence subsequent practice and training across the department.

What should a departmental policy contain?

The starting points for your departmental SEND policy will be the whole-school SEND policy and the SEND Information Report that, under the Children and Families Act 2014, all schools are required to publish. Each subject department's own policy should then flesh out the detail in a way that describes how things will work in practice. Writing the policy needs to be much more than a paper exercise completed merely to satisfy the senior management team and Ofsted inspectors. Rather, it is an opportunity for your staff to come together as a team to create a framework for teaching science in a way that makes your subject accessible, not only to pupils with special educational needs and disabilities, but for all pupils in the school. It is also an ideal opportunity to discuss the impact of grouping on academic and social outcomes for pupils. (Bear in mind that the SEND Code of Practice includes a specific duty that 'schools must ensure that pupils with SEND engage in the activities of the school alongside pupils who do not have SEND' (6.2, p. 92).

We need to be careful in science that when grouping pupils, we are not bound solely by measures in reading and writing, but also take into account reasoning and oral language abilities. It is vital that social issues are also taken into account if pupils are to be able to learn effectively. Having a complement of pupils with good oral ability will lift the attitude and attainment of everybody within a group.

Who should be involved in developing our SEND policy?

The job of developing and reviewing your policy will be easier if tackled as a joint endeavour. Involve people who will be able to offer support and guidance such as:

- The school SEND governor
- The SENCO or other school leader with responsibility for SEND
- Your support staff, including teaching assistants and technicians
- The school data manager who will be able to offer information about the attainment and progress of different groups
- Outside experts from your local authority, academy chain or other schools
- Parents of pupils with SEND
- Pupils themselves – both with and without SEND

Bringing together a range of views and information will enable you to develop a policy that is compliant with the letter **and** principle of the legislation, that is relevant to the context of your school and that is useful in guiding practice and improving outcomes for all pupils.

The role of parents in developing your department SEND policy

As outlined in Appendix 1, Section 19 of the Children and Families Act 2014 raises the bar of expectations about how parents should be involved in and influence the work of schools. Not only is it best practice to involve parents of pupils with SEND in the development of policy, but it will also help in 'getting it right' for both pupils and staff. There are a number of ways, both formal and informal, to find out the views of parents to inform policy writing, including:

- Focus group
- Coffee morning/drop-in
- Questionnaire/online survey
- Phone survey of a sample of parents

Parents will often respond more readily if the request for feedback or invitation to attend a meeting comes from their son or daughter.

Where to start when writing a policy

An audit can act as a starting point for reviewing current policy on SEND or writing a new policy. This will involve gathering information and reviewing current practice with regard to pupils with SEND and is best completed by the whole department, preferably with some input from the SENCO or another member of staff with responsibility for SEND within the school. An audit carried out by the whole department provides a valuable opportunity for professional development so long as it is seen as an exercise in sharing good practice and encourages joint planning. It may also facilitate your department's contribution to the school provision map. But before embarking on an audit, it is worth investing some time in a departmental meeting, or ideally a training day, to raise awareness of the legislation around special educational needs and disabilities and to establish a shared philosophy across your department.

The following headings may be useful when you are establishing your departmental policy:

General statement of compliance

- What is the overarching aim of the policy? What outcomes do you want to achieve for pupils with SEND?
- How are you complying with legislation and guidance?
- What does the school SEND Information Report say about teaching and learning and provision for pupils with SEND?

Example

All members of the department will ensure that the needs of all pupils with SEND are met according to the aims of the schools and its SEND policy. . .

Definition of SEND

- What does SEND mean?
- What are the areas of need and the categories used in the Code of Practice?
- Are there any special implications for our subject area?

(See Chapter 1.)

Provision for staff within the department

- Who has responsibility for SEND within the department?
- What are the responsibilities of this role?

e.g.

- Liaison between the department and the SENCO
- Monitoring the progress of and outcomes for pupils with SEND, e.g., identifying attainment gaps between pupils with SEND and their peers
- Attending any liaison meetings and providing feedback to colleagues
- Attending and contributing to training
- Maintaining departmental SEND information and records
- Representing the needs of pupils with SEND at the departmental level
- Liaising with parents of pupils with SEND
- Gathering feedback from pupils with SEND on the impact of teaching and support strategies on their learning and well-being

(This post can be seen as a valuable development opportunity for staff, and the name of this person should be included in the policy. However, where responsibility for SEND is given to a relatively junior member of the team, there must be support and supervision from the head of the department to ensure that the needs of pupils with SEND have sufficient prominence in both policy and practice.)

- What information about pupils' SEND is held, where is it stored and how is it shared?
- How can staff access additional resources, information and training?
- How will staff ensure effective planning and communication between teachers and teaching assistants?
- What assessments are available for teachers in your department to support accurate identification of SEND?

Example

The member of staff with responsibility for overseeing the provision of SEND within the department will attend liaison meetings and subsequently give feedback to the other members of the department. S/he will maintain the department's SEND file, attend and/or organise appropriate training and disseminate this to all departmental staff. All information will be treated with confidentiality.

Provision for pupils with SEND

How are pupils' special educational needs identified?

e.g.

- Observation in lessons
- Assessment of class work/homework
- End of module tests/progress checks
- Annual examinations/SATs/GCSE
- Reports

How is progress measured for pupils with SEND?

How do members of the department contribute to individual learning plans, meetings with parents and reviews?

What criteria are used for organising teaching groups?

How/when can pupils move between groups?

What adjustments are made for pupils with special educational needs and/or disabilities in lessons and homework?

How do we use information about pupils' abilities in reading, writing, speaking and listening when planning lessons and homework?

What alternative courses are available for pupils with SEND?

What special arrangements are made for internal and external examinations?

What guidance is available for working effectively with support staff?

Here is a good place also to put a statement about the school behaviour policy and any rewards and sanctions and how the department will make any necessary adjustments to meet the needs of pupils with SEND.

Example

The staff in the [subject] department will aim to support pupils with SEND to achieve the best possible outcomes. They will do this by supporting pupils to achieve their individual targets as specified in their individual learning plans, and the staff will provide feedback for progress reviews. Pupils with SEND will be included in the departmental monitoring system used for all pupils.

Resources and learning materials

- Is any specialist equipment used in the department?
- How are differentiated resources developed? What criteria do we use (e.g., literacy levels)?
- Where are resources stored, and are they accessible for both staff and pupils?

Example

The department will provide suitably differentiated materials and, where appropriate, specialist resources to meet the needs of pupils with SEND. Alternative courses and examinations will be made available where appropriate for individual pupils. Support staff will be provided with curriculum information in advance of lessons and will be involved in lesson planning. A list of resources is available in the department handbook.

Staff qualifications and continuing professional development (CPD)

- What qualifications and experience do the members of the department have?
- What training has already taken place, and when? What impact did that training have on teaching and learning, as well as progress, for pupils with SEND?
- How is training planned? What criteria are used to identify training needs?
- How is SEND taken into account when new training opportunities are proposed?
- Is a record kept of training completed and on-going training needs?

Example

A record of training undertaken, specialist skills and training required will be kept in the department handbook. Requests for training will be considered in line with the department and school improvement plan.

Monitoring and reviewing the policy

- How will the policy be monitored?
- Who will lead the monitoring?
- When will the policy be reviewed?

Example

The department SEND policy will be monitored by the Head of Department on a planned annual basis, with advice being sought from the SENCO as part of the three-yearly review process.

Conclusion

Creating a departmental SEND policy should be a developmental activity that will improve teaching and learning for all pupils, but especially for those who are vulnerable to underachievement. The policy should be a working document that will evolve and change over time; it is there to challenge current practice and to encourage improvement for both pupils and staff. If departmental staff work together to create the policy, they will have ownership of it; it will have true meaning and will be effective in clarifying good practice.

 An example of a departmental policy for you to amend is available on the dedicated website www.routledge.com/9781138209053.

Appendix 1.3   Different types of SEND

Introduction

This appendix is a starting point for information on the special educational needs most frequently encountered in mainstream schools. It describes the main characteristics of each area of special educational need and disability with practical ideas for use in science, and contacts for further information.

There is a measure of repetition, as some strategies prove to be effective with a whole range of pupils (and often with those who have no identified SEND!). However, the layout enables readers an 'at a glance' reminder of effective approaches and facilitates copying for colleagues and TAs.

The SEND Code of Practice (DfE 2015) outlines four broad areas of need. These are:

- Communication and interaction
- Cognition and learning
- Social, emotional and mental health difficulties
- Sensory and/or physical needs

These broad areas are not exclusive, and pupils may have needs that cut across some or all of them. Equally, pupils' difficulties and needs will change over time. The terms used in this book are helpful when reviewing and monitoring special educational provision, but pupils' individual talents and interests are just as important as their disability or special educational need. Because of this, specific terms or labels need to be used with care in discussion with parents, pupils or other professionals. Unless a pupil has a firm diagnosis, and parents and pupil understand the implications of that diagnosis, it is more appropriate to describe the features of the special educational need rather than use the label. For example a teacher might describe a pupil's spelling difficulties but not use the term 'dyslexic'.

There is a continuum of need within each of the special educational needs and disabilities listed here. Some pupils will be affected more than others and may show fewer or more of the characteristics described.

Pupils with other, less common special educational needs may be included in some schools, and additional information on these conditions may be found in a variety of sources. These include the school SENCO, local authority support services, educational psychologists and online information, for example on the Nasen SEND Gateway and disability charity websites such as Mencap, CAF or I CAN, the Children's Communication Charity.

---

www.nasen.org.uk

www.mencap.org.uk

www.cafamily.org.uk

www.ican.org.uk

Attention deficit disorder (with or without hyperactivity) ADD/ADHD

Attention deficit hyperactivity disorder is one of the most common childhood disorders and can continue through adolescence and adulthood. ADHD can occur in pupils of any intellectual ability and may also cause additional problems, such as sleep and anxiety disorders. The features of ADHD usually diminish with age, but many individuals who are diagnosed with the condition at a young age will continue to experience problems in adulthood.

Main characteristics

- Short attention span or easily distracted by noise and movement
- Difficulty in following instructions and completing tasks
- Difficulty in listening to and processing verbal instructions
- Restlessness and inability to keep still, causing frequent fidgeting
- Difficulty with moderating behaviour such as constant talking, interrupting and calling out
- Difficulty in waiting or taking turns
- Impulsivity – acting without thinking about consequences

How can the science teacher help?

- Make eye contact and use the pupil's name when speaking to him or her.
- Keep instructions simple – the one-sentence rule.
- Provide clear written instruction.
- Position the pupil away from obvious distractions, e.g., windows, computer screens.
- Provide clear routines and rules, and rehearse them regularly.
- Encourage the pupil to repeat instructions (to you or TA) before starting work.
- Tell the pupil when to begin a task.
- Give two choices – avoid the option of the pupil saying no: e.g., 'Do you want to write in blue or black pen?'
- Give advance warning when something is about to happen. Signal a change or finish with a time, e.g., 'In two minutes I need you to. . .'
- Give specific praise – catch the pupil being good, give attention for positive behaviour.
- Give the pupil responsibilities so others can see him or her in a positive light and the pupil can develop a positive self-image.

ADDISS 020 8952 2800 www.addiss.co.uk

ADHD Foundation 0151 237 2661 www.adhdfoundation.org.uk

Young Minds 020 7089 5050 www.youngminds.org.uk

Autism (ASD)

Asperger syndrome

Asperger syndrome is a type of autism. People with Asperger syndrome do not have 'learning difficulties' as such, but they do have difficulties associated with being on the autistic spectrum. They often want to make friends but do not understand the complex rules of social interaction. They may have impaired fine and gross motor skills, with writing being a particular problem. Boys are more likely to be affected – with the ratio being 10:1 boys to girls. Because they appear 'odd' and naïve, these pupils are particularly vulnerable to bullying.

Main characteristics

- **Social interaction**
  Pupils with Asperger syndrome want friends but have not developed the strategies necessary for making and sustaining meaningful friendships. They find it very difficult to learn social norms and to pick up on social cues. Social situations, such as assemblies and less formal lessons, can cause great anxiety.

- **Social communication**
  Pupils have appropriate spoken language but tend to sound formal and pedantic, using limited expression and possibly with an unusual tone of voice. They have difficulty using and understanding non-verbal language such as facial expression, gesture, body language and eye contact. They may have a literal understanding of language and do not grasp implied meanings.

- **Social imagination**
  Pupils with Asperger syndrome need structured environments and routines they understand and can anticipate. They may excel at learning facts but have difficulty understanding abstract concepts and generalising information and skills. They often have all-consuming special interests.

How can the science teacher help?

- Liaise with parents, especially over homework.
- Create as calm a classroom environment as possible.
- Allow to sit in the same place for each lesson.
- Set up a 'work buddy' system for your lessons.
- Provide additional visual cues in class, such as visual timetables and task activity lists.
- Give the pupils time to process questions and respond.
- Make sure pupils understand what you expect of them.
- Offer alternatives to handwriting for recording work.

- Prepare pupils for changes to routines well in advance.
- Give written homework instructions.
- Have your own class/laboratory rules and apply them consistently.

Autism spectrum disorder (ASD)

Autism is a developmental disability that affects how people communicate with, and relate to, other people. It also affects how they make sense of the world around them. It is often referred to as a spectrum, or ASD, which means that, while all people with autism share certain difficulties, the condition may affect them in different ways. Pupils with ASD cover the full range of academic ability, and the severity of the disability varies widely. Some pupils also have learning disabilities or other difficulties, such as dyslexia. Four times as many boys as girls are diagnosed with an ASD.

Main characteristics

- **Social interaction**
  Pupils with ASD find it difficult to understand social behaviour, and this affects their ability to interact with others. They do not always understand social contexts. They may experience high levels of stress and anxiety in settings that do not meet their needs or when routines are changed. This can lead to inappropriate behaviour.

- **Social communication**
  Understanding and use of non-verbal and verbal communication are impaired. Pupils with an ASD have difficulty understanding the communication of others and developing effective communication themselves. They may have a literal understanding of language. Many are delayed in learning to speak, and some people with ASD never develop speech at all.

- **Social imagination and flexibility of thought**
  Pupils with an ASD have difficulty thinking and behaving flexibly, which may result in restricted, obsessional or repetitive activities. They are often more interested in objects than people and have intense interests in such things as trains and vacuum cleaners. Pupils work best when they have a routine. Unexpected changes in those routines will cause distress.

  Some pupils with autistic spectrum disorders have a different perception of sounds, sights, smell, touch and taste, and this can affect their response to these sensations.

How can the science teacher help?

- Collaborate closely with parents as they will have many useful strategies.
- Provide visual supports in class; objects, pictures, a symbol timetable, etc.

- Always consider potential sensory issues.
- Give advance warning of any changes to usual routines.
- Provide either an individual desk or the opportunity to work with a 'buddy'.
- Give individual instructions using the pupil's name at the beginning of the request, e.g., 'Paul, bring me your book'.
- Be alert to pupils' levels of anxiety.
- Develop social interactions using a buddy system or circle of friends.
- Avoid using metaphor, idiom or sarcasm – say what you mean in simple language.
- Use pupils' special interests as motivations.
- Help pupils manage potentially difficult situations by rehearsing them beforehand (perhaps with a TA) or through the use of social stories.

- The National Autistic Society 020 7833 2299 www.autism.org.uk

- Autism Education Trust 0207 903 3650
  www.autismeducationtrust.org.uk

Cerebral palsy (CP)

Cerebral palsy is a condition that affects muscle control and movement. It is usually caused by an injury to the brain before, during or after birth. Pupils with cerebral palsy have difficulties controlling their muscles and movements as they grow and develop. Problems vary from slight clumsiness to more severe lack of control of movements. Pupils with CP may also have learning difficulties. They may use a wheelchair or other mobility aid.

Main characteristics

There are three main forms of cerebral palsy:

- **Spastic cerebral palsy** – associated with stiff or tight muscle tone resulting in a decreased range of movement. This stiffening of muscle tone can be very painful and can affect different parts of the body.
- **Dyskenetic cerebral palsy** – sustained or intermittent involuntary muscle contractions often affecting the whole body.
- **Ataxic cerebral palsy** – an inability to activate the correct pattern of muscles during movement, resulting in an unsteady gait with balance difficulties and poor spatial awareness.

Pupils with CP may also have communication difficulties.

How can the science teacher help?

- Gather information from parents and therapists involved with the pupil (perhaps via the SENCO until parents' evening provides an opportunity for a face-to-face chat).
- Consider the classroom layout to maximise access.
- Have high academic expectations.
- Use visual supports; objects, pictures, symbols.
- Arrange for a work or science buddy.
- Speak directly to the pupil rather than through a teaching assistant.
- Ensure access to appropriate IT equipment for the science – and check that it is used effectively.
- Adapt, as necessary, any equipment that is needed for practical work.

Scope 0808 800 3333 www.scope.org.uk

Down syndrome

Down syndrome (DS) is the most common identifiable cause of learning disability. This is a genetic condition caused by the presence of an extra chromosome 21. People with DS have varying degrees of learning difficulties ranging from mild to severe. They have a specific learning profile with characteristic strengths and weaknesses. All share certain physical characteristics but will also inherit family traits, in physical features and personality. They may have additional sight, hearing, respiratory and heart problems.

Main characteristics

- Delayed motor skills
- Taking longer to learn and consolidate new skills
- Limited concentration
- Difficulties with generalisation, thinking and reasoning
- Sequencing difficulties
- Stronger visual than aural skills
- Better social than academic skills

How can the science teacher help?

- Ensure that the pupil can see and hear you and other pupils.
- Speak directly to the pupil and reinforce speech with facial expression, pictures and objects.
- Use simple, familiar language in short sentences.
- Check that instructions have been understood.
- Give the pupil time to process information and formulate a response.
- Break lessons up into a series of shorter, varied and achievable tasks.
- Accept alternative ways of responding to tasks; drawings, audio or video recordings, symbols, etc.
- Set individual tasks linked to the work of the rest of the class.
- Provide age-appropriate resources and activities.
- Allow the pupil to work with more able peers to give good models of work and behaviour.
- Provide a work buddy.
- Expect pupil to work unsupported for part of every lesson to avoid over-dependence on adult support.
- Provide adapted equipment for practical work where appropriate.

Down's Syndrome Association 020 8682400 www.downs-syndrome.org.uk

Foetal alcohol syndrome

Foetal alcohol syndrome (FAS), or foetal alcohol spectrum disorders (FASD), are umbrella terms for diagnoses relating to a child's exposure to alcohol before birth. Alcohol can affect the development of all cells and organs, but it is the brain and nervous system that are particularly vulnerable. Each person with FAS/D may face a range of difficulties across a spectrum from mild to severe.

Main characteristics

- Visual impairment
- Sleep problems
- Speech and language delay
- Impulsivity and/or hyperactivity
- Memory problems
- Inappropriate social behaviour

How can the science teacher help?

- Gather information from parents and other professionals involved with the pupil to find the most effective ways of teaching him or her (perhaps through the SENCO in the first instance).
- Find out the pupil's strengths and use these as starting points for learning.
- Keep instructions simple, and offer information in verbal and visual form.
- Ensure class routines are explicit and followed consistently.
- Use concrete and positive language, e.g., 'Walk' rather than 'Don't run'.
- Check that the pupil knows and understands any school or class rules.
- Specify clearly what is expected for any task or activity.
- Provide a memory mat or audio recording facilities to support retention of information, e.g., homework tasks, spelling, etc.

Learning disability (learning difficulty)

The terms 'learning disability' and 'learning difficulty' are used to describe a wide continuum of difficulties ranging from moderate (MLD) to profound and multiple (PMLD). Pupils with learning disabilities find it harder to understand, learn and remember new things, meaning they may have problems across a range of areas such as communication, being aware of risks or managing everyday tasks.

Moderate learning difficulties (MLD)

The term 'moderate learning difficulties' is used to describe pupils who find it extremely difficult to achieve expected levels of attainment across the curriculum, even with a well-differentiated and flexible approach to teaching. These pupils do not find learning easy and can suffer from low self-esteem and sometimes exhibit unacceptable behaviour as a way of avoiding failure. For all pupils with learning disabilities, the social aspect of school is a crucial element in their development and understanding of the 'culture' of young people, so it is important for them to have friends who don't have learning disabilities as well as those who do. As the SEND Code of Practice says at 6.2 (p. 92): 'Schools must. . . ensure that children and young people with SEN engage in the activities of the school alongside pupils who do not have SEN'.

Main characteristics

- Difficulties with reading, writing and comprehension
- Problems understanding and retaining mathematical skills and concepts
- Immature social and emotional skills
- Limited vocabulary and communication skills
- Short attention span
- Underdeveloped coordination skills
- Inability to transfer and apply skills to different situations
- Difficulty remembering what has been taught previously
- Difficulty with personal organisation such as following a timetable, remembering books and equipment

How can the science teacher help?

- Find out about the pupil's strengths, interest and areas of weaknesses.
- Have high expectations.
- Establish a routine within your lessons.
- Keep tasks short and varied.
- Keep listening tasks short or broken up with other activities.
- Provide word lists, writing frames and shortened versions of text to be read.

- Offer alternative methods of recording information, e.g., drawings, charts, labelling, diagrams, use of IT.
- Check previously gained knowledge and build on this (it may be at a very different level to other pupils in the class).
- Offer instructions and information in different ways.
- Be explicit about the expected outcome; demonstrate or show examples of completed work.
- Use practical, concrete, visual examples to illustrate explanations.
- Question the pupil to check that he or she has grasped a concept or has understood instructions.
- Make sure the pupil always has something to do.
- Use lots of praise, instant rewards, catch them trying hard.
- Provide adapted equipment for practical work where appropriate.

Severe learning difficulties (SLD)

This term covers a wide and varied group of pupils who have significant intellectual or cognitive impairments. Many have communication difficulties and/ or sensory impairments in addition to more general learning difficulties. Some pupils may also have difficulties in mobility, coordination and perception, and the use of signs and symbols will be helpful to support their communication and understanding. Pupils' academic attainment will also vary, with many able to access a well-differentiated mainstream curriculum and achieve at GCSE level.

How can the science teacher help?

- Liaise with parents (perhaps through the SENCO in the first instance).
- Arrange a work/science buddy.
- Use visual supports: objects, pictures, symbols.
- Learn some signs relevant to the teaching of science.
- Allow time for pupils to process information and formulate responses.
- Set differentiated tasks linked to the work of the rest of the class.
- Set achievable targets for each lesson or module of work.
- Accept different recording methods; drawings, audio or video recordings, photographs, etc.
- Give access to computers where appropriate.
- Plan a series of short, varied activities within each lesson.
- Provide adapted equipment for practical work where appropriate.

Profound and multiple learning difficulties (PMLD)

Pupils with profound and multiple learning difficulties have complex learning needs. In addition to severe learning difficulties, pupils have other significant difficulties, such as physical disabilities, sensory impairments or severe medical conditions. Pupils with PMLD require a high level of adult support, both for their learning needs and for personal care.

Pupils with PMLD are able to access the curriculum largely through sensory experiences. Some pupils communicate by gesture, eye pointing or symbols, others by very simple language. The concept of progress for pupils with PMLD covers more than academic attainment. Indeed, for some pupils who may have associated medical conditions, simply maintaining knowledge and skills will count as good progress.

How can the science teacher help?

- Work closely with teaching/support assistants working with the pupil.
- Consider the classroom layout so that wheelchairs can move around easily and safely.
- Identify all possible sensory opportunities in your lessons.
- Use additional sensory supports: objects, pictures, fragrances, music, textures, food, etc.
- Use photographs to record the pupil's experiences and responses.
- Set up a work/science buddy rota for the class.
- Identify opportunities for the pupil to work in groups.

Mencap 020 7454 0454 www.mencap.org.uk

Foundation for People with Learning Disabilities 020 7803 1100 www.learningdisabilities.org.uk

---

Physical disability (PD)

There are a wide range of physical disabilities, and pupils with PD span all academic abilities. Some pupils are able to access the curriculum and learn effectively without additional educational provision. They have a disability but do not have a special educational need. For other pupils, the impact of their disability on their education may be significant, and the school will need to make adjustments to enable access to the curriculum.

Some pupils with a physical disability have associated medical conditions that may have an impact on their mobility. These conditions include cerebral palsy, heart disease, spina bifida and muscular dystrophy. They may also have sensory impairments, neurological problems or learning disabilities. They may use a wheelchair and/or additional mobility aids. Some pupils will be mobile but may have significant fine motor difficulties that require support or specialist resources. Others may need augmentative or alternative communication aids.

Pupils with a physical disability may need to miss lessons to attend physiotherapy or medical appointments. They are also likely to become very tired as they expend greater effort to complete everyday tasks. Teachers need to be flexible and sensitive to individual pupil needs.

How can the science teacher help?

- Get to know the pupil (and parents) so that they will help you make the right adjustments.
- Maintain high expectations.
- Consider the classroom layout.
- Give permission for the pupil to leave lessons a few minutes early to avoid busy corridors and have time to get to next lesson.
- Set homework earlier in the lesson so instructions are not missed.
- Speak directly to pupil rather than through a teaching assistant.
- Let pupils make their own decisions.
- Ensure access to appropriate IT equipment for the lesson – and check that it is used.
- Provide adapted equipment for practical work where appropriate.
- Offer alternative ways of recording work.
- Plan to cover work missed through illness or medical appointments.
- Be sensitive to fatigue, especially towards the end of the school day.

Scope 0808 800 3333 www.scope.org.uk

Social, emotional and mental health difficulties

This area includes pupils who experience a wide range of difficulties characterised in a number of ways, including becoming withdrawn or exhibiting behavioural difficulties. Behaviours such as these may reflect underlying mental health difficulties including depression, anxiety and eating disorders. These difficulties can be seen across the whole ability range and have a continuum of severity. Attachment disorders and attention deficit disorder will also be part of this continuum. Pupils with special educational needs in this area are those who have persistent difficulties despite the school having in place an effective school behaviour policy and a robust personal and social curriculum.

Main characteristics

- Inattentive, poor concentration and lacking interest in school and schoolwork
- Easily frustrated and anxious about changes
- Difficulty working in groups
- Unable to work independently, constantly seeking help or attention
- Confrontational: verbally aggressive towards pupils and/or adults
- Physically aggressive towards pupils and/or adults
- Destroys property: their own and that of others
- Appears withdrawn, distressed, unhappy, or sulky and may self-harm
- Lacks confidence and self-esteem
- May find it difficult to communicate
- Finds it difficult to accept praise

How can the science teacher help?

- Check the ability level of the pupil and adapt expectations of work accordingly.
- Consider the pupil's strengths and interests and use these as motivators.
- Tell the pupil clearly what you expect in advance for work and for behaviour.
- Talk to the pupil to find out more about him or her and how the pupil feels about learning.
- Set a science target with a reward system.
- Focus your comments on the behaviour not on the pupil ('That was a rude thing to say' rather than 'You are a rude boy').
- Use positive language and gestures and verbal praise whenever possible.
- Tell the pupil what you want them to do, 'I need you to. . .', 'I want you to. . .', rather than ask, 'Will you?' This avoids confrontation and the possibility that there is room for negotiation.
- Give the pupil a choice between two options.
- Stick to what you say. Be consistent.
- Give the pupil class responsibilities to increase self-esteem and confidence.
- Plan a 'time out' system. Ask a colleague for help with this.

SEBDA 01233 622958 www.sebda.org

Sensory impairments

Hearing impairment (HI)

The term 'hearing impairment' is a generic term used to describe all hearing loss. The main types of loss are monaural, conductive, sensory and mixed loss. The degree of hearing loss is described as mild, moderate, severe or profound.

How can the science teacher help?

- Find out about the degree of the pupil's hearing loss and the likely implications for your lessons.
- Allocate the most appropriate seating position for the pupil (e g., away from the hum of computers, with the better ear towards speaker).
- Check that the pupil can see your face for facial expressions and lip reading.
- Make sure the light falls on your face and lips. Do not stand with your back to a window.
- Provide a list of vocabulary, context and visual clues, especially for new sciences.
- During class discussion allow one pupil to speak at a time and indicate where the speaker is.
- Check that any aids are working.
- If you use interactive whiteboards, ensure that the beam does not prevent the pupil from seeing your face.

Action on Hearing Loss 020 7296 8000 www.actiononhearingloss.org.uk

The National Deaf Children's Society 020 7490 8656 www.ndcs.org.uk

---

Visual impairment (VI)

Visual impairment refers to a range of difficulties and includes the disabilities of those pupils with monocular vision (vision in one eye), those who are partially sighted and those who are blind. Pupils with visual impairment cover the whole ability range, and some pupils may have additional special educational needs.

How can the science teacher help?

- Check the optimum position for the pupil, e g., for a monocular pupil, his or her good eye should be towards the action.
- Always provide the pupil with his or her own copy of any texts, with enlarged print where possible.
- Check accessibility of IT systems (enlarged icons, screen readers, etc.).
- Do not stand with your back to the window as this creates a silhouette and makes it harder for the pupil to see you.
- Draw the pupil's attention to displays – which he or she may not notice.
- Make sure the floor is kept free of clutter.
- Let the pupil know if there is a change to the layout of a space.
- Ask if there is any specialist equipment that the pupil requires for your science, such as enlarged print dictionaries or additional lighting.
- Provide adapted equipment for practical work where appropriate.

Royal National Institute for Blind People (RNIB) 0303 123 9999
www.rnib.org.uk

Multi-sensory impairment (MSI)

Pupils with multi-sensory impairment have a combination of visual and hearing difficulties. They may also have other additional disabilities that make their situation complex. A pupil with these difficulties is likely to need a high level of individual support.

How can the science teacher help?

- Liaise with specialist teachers and support staff to ascertain the appropriate provision within your science.
- Learn how to use alternative means of communication, as appropriate.
- Be prepared to be flexible and to adapt tasks, targets and assessment procedures.

Specific learning difficulties (SpLD)

The term 'specific learning difficulties' includes dyslexia, dyscalculia and dyspraxia.

Dyslexia

The term 'dyslexia' is used to describe difficulties that affect the ability to learn to read, write and/or spell stemming from a difficulty in processing the sounds in words. Although found across a whole range of ability, pupils with dyslexia often have strengths in reasoning and in visual and creative skills, but their particular difficulties can result in underachievement in school. While pupils can learn strategies to manage the effects of dyslexia, it is a life-long condition, and its effects may be amplified at times of stress or in unfamiliar situations.

Main characteristics of dyslexia

- The pupil may frequently lose his or her place while reading, make errors with even high-frequency words and have difficulty reading names, blending sounds and segmenting words. Reading and writing require a great deal of effort and concentration.
- Written work may seem messy, with uneven letters and crossings out. Similarly shaped letters may be confused, such as *b/d/p/q*, *m/w*, *n/u*, and letters in words may be jumbled, such as *tired/tried*. Spelling difficulties often persist into adult life, and these pupils can become reluctant writers.
- Personal organisation can be underdeveloped.

How can the science teacher help?

- Be aware of the pupil's individual strengths and areas of difficulty – speak to him or her directly to identify effective support strategies.
- Teach and encourage the use of IT, such as spell-checkers, predictive text, screen readers, etc.
- Provide word lists and photocopies rather than expect the pupil to copy from the board.
- Consider alternatives to lengthy pieces of writing, e g., pictures, plans, flow charts, mind maps, podcasts, etc.
- Allow extra time for tasks including assessments and examinations.
- Support the pupil in recording homework to be completed – and time scales.

Dyscalculia

The term 'dyscalculia' is used to describe difficulties in processing number concepts and mastering basic numeracy skills. These difficulties might be in marked contrast to the pupil's developmental level and general ability in other areas.

Main characteristics of dyscalculia

- The pupil may have difficulty counting by rote or writing or reading numbers, miss out or reverse numbers, have difficulty with mental maths, and be unable to remember concepts, rules and formulae.
- In maths-based concepts, the pupil may have difficulty with money, telling the time, giving/following directions, using right and left and sequencing events. He or she may also be prone to losing track of turn-taking, e.g., in team games or dance.
- Poor time management and organisation skills.

How can the science teacher help?

- Provide number/word/rule/formulae lists, etc. rather than expect the pupil to copy from the board. (Credit card holders can be useful for keeping reminders close at hand to aid memory.)
- Make full use of IT to support learning.
- Encourage the use of rough paper for working out.
- Check understanding at regular intervals.
- Offer a framework for setting out work.
- Provide concrete, practical objects that are appropriate for the pupil's age.
- Allow extra time for tasks including assessments and examinations.

Dyspraxia

Dyspraxia is a common developmental disorder that affects fine and gross motor coordination and may also affect speech. The pattern of coordination difficulties will vary from person to person and will affect participation and functioning in everyday life as well as in school.

Main characteristics of dyspraxia

- Difficulty in coordinating movements, making pupils appear clumsy
- Difficulty with handwriting and drawing, throwing and catching
- Confusion between left and right
- Difficulty following sequences and multiple instructions
- Weak grasp of spatial concepts; in, above, behind, etc.
- May misinterpret situations, take things literally
- Limited social skills resulting in frustration and irritability
- Possible articulation difficulties

How can the science teacher help?

- Be sensitive to the pupil's limitations in games and practical/outdoor activities and plan tasks to enable success.
- Limit the amount of writing expected.

- Ask the pupil questions to check his or her understanding of instructions/ tasks.
- Check the pupil's seating position to encourage good presentation (both feet resting on the floor, desk at elbow height and, ideally, with a sloping surface on which to work).
- Provide adapted equipment for practical work where appropriate.

Dyspraxia Foundation 01462 455 016 www.dyspraxiafoundation.org.uk

Speech, language and communication difficulties (SLCD)

Pupils with speech, language and communication difficulties have problems that affect the full range of communication, and the development of skills may be significantly delayed. Such difficulties are very common in young children, but most problems are resolved during the primary years. Problems that persist beyond the transfer to secondary school will be more severe and will have a significant effect on self-esteem and personal and social relationships. The development of literacy skills is also likely to be affected. Even where pupils learn to decode, they may not understand what they have read. Sign language and symbols offer pupils an additional method of communication.

Pupils with speech, language and communication difficulties cover the whole range of academic abilities.

Main characteristics

- Speech difficulties: difficulties with expressive language may involve problems in articulation and the production of speech sounds or in coordinating the muscles that control speech. Pupils may have a stammer or some other form of dysfluency.
- Language/communication difficulties: receptive language impairments lead to difficulty in understanding other people. Pupils may use words incorrectly with inappropriate grammatical patterns, have a reduced vocabulary or find it hard to recall words and express ideas. Some pupils will also have difficulty using and understanding eye contact, facial expression, gesture and body language.

How can the science teacher help?

- Gather information about the pupil (perhaps via the SENCO) and talk to the pupil him- or herself about strategies to provide support in your science.
- Use visual supports such as objects, pictures and symbols.
- Use the pupil's name when addressing him or her to alert the pupil to a question or instruction.
- Give one instruction at a time, using short sentences.
- Give pupils time to respond before repeating a question.
- Provide a good model of spoken language and rephrase pupil's response where appropriate: 'I think you are saying that. . .'
- Make sure pupils understand what they have to do before expecting them to start a task.
- Pair with a work/science buddy.
- Give access to a computer or other IT equipment appropriate to the science.
- Give written homework instructions.

I CAN 0845 225 4073 or 020 7843 2552 www.ican.org.uk

AFASIC 0300 666 9410 (Helpline) www.afasic.org.uk

Tourette syndrome (TS)

Tourette syndrome is a neurological disorder characterised by 'tics' – involuntary rapid or sudden movements or sounds that are frequently repeated. There is a wide range of severity of the condition, with some people having no need to seek medical help whilst others have a socially disabling condition. The tics can be suppressed for a short time but will be more noticeable when the pupil is anxious or excited.

Main characteristics

Physical tics range from simple blinking or nodding through more complex movements and conditions such as echopraxia (imitating actions seen) or copropraxia (repeatedly making obscene gestures).

Vocal tics may be as simple as throat clearing or coughing but can progress to be as extreme as echolalia (the repetition of what was last heard) or coprolalia (the repetition of obscene words).

TS itself causes no behavioural or educational problems, but pupils may also have other associated disorders such as attention deficit hyperactivity disorder (ADHD) or obsessive compulsive disorder (OCD).

How can the science teacher help?

- Establish a good rapport with the pupil.
- Talk to the class about TS and establish an understanding and tolerant ethos.
- Agree an 'escape route' signal should the tics become overwhelming for the pupil or disruptive for the rest of the class.
- Allow pupil to sit at the back of the room to be less obvious.
- Give access to a computer to reduce the need for handwriting.
- Make sure pupil is not teased or bullied.
- Be alert for signs of anxiety or depression.

Tourettes Action UK 0300 777 8427 (Helpdesk) www.tourettes-action.org.uk

Appendix 2.1 SEND training for science staff

Some questions to consider when creating an inclusive learning environment

- What is it like to live with certain disabilities?
- How does each of these affect the pupil's ability to carry out simple experiments?
- How can we modify the laboratory to help these pupils?
- How do we modify teaching materials to support these pupils?
- How do we modify apparatus to support these pupils?
- Do we need any other apparatus or resources?

Simulating disabilities

It is rarely possible to simulate disabilities so that your experience is exactly the same as the pupil's. Coping with a disability for a short period is completely different from coping with this every day of your life. However, it makes us more aware if we simulate and try to experience these difficulties.

Visual impairment

Wrap cling film or bubble wrap unevenly round a pair of goggles to restrict vision.

Now set up a microscope and dissect a flower, look at the anthers and observe the pollen grains.

How did you feel?

You have to do everything wearing the goggles.

Physical disabilities

Bind your index and middle fingers together on both hands.

Now collect and test the pH of 3 solutions with pH paper.

Now do the same but use a pH meter.

Which method was easier?

Hearing impairment

Make a tape with low-level background noise, such as running water, music, etc., and the occasional loud noise, and over the top of this give some verbal instructions.

Ask another member of your department to listen to the tape and write the instructions down.

Collect the following feedback:

- How easy was it to write the instructions down?
- Which of the noises caused most distraction?
- How could you make it easier for this pupil to receive these instructions?

Summing up

- What were the difficulties you encountered?
- How could these have been overcome to make access to the science better?
- How could we improve access to the curriculum for our pupils with SEN?

Appendix 2.2   Worksheet – Stopping rust

Name:	Date:	Class:

You need to collect:

4 iron nails	salt water
4 test tubes (numbered 1–4)	paint
Grease	strips of zinc

What to do:

1   Paint one nail and let it dry.
2   Put grease on the second nail.
3   Wrap a strip of zinc around the third nail.
4   The last nail can be used as it is.
5   Put the test tubes into a rack and put one nail in each.
6   Pour salt water into the test tubes to cover the nails.
7   Leave the test tubes for a week, then look to see what has happened.

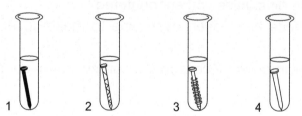

Write down your results

Nail:	What the nail looks like after one week in the salt water:
1 painted	
2 greased	
3 zinc covered	
4 untreated	

What does this show?

Which is the best way to stop iron from going rusty?

Appendix 2.3　Writing frame 1 – Planning an investigation

_____

This is the apparatus I will need:

This is what I will do:

This is what I will do to make the experiment a fair test:

This is what I will do to make it safe:
_____

_____

If I change..., the variable, my prediction will be:

Prediction: What I think will happen is:

This is because:
_____

By using Clicker, some phrases could be put in the boxes, and then the pupil will only have to move them by clicking on them.

Appendix 2.4   Presenting my results

Now that I have my results, how will I present them?

I could draw a pie chart like this one using my results. I will need to give it a title and label the parts.

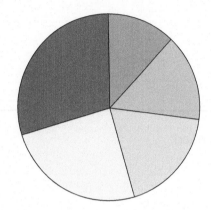

I could draw a bar chart like this with my results. I will need to label the axes.

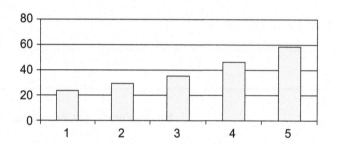

I could draw a line graph. I will need to give it a title and label the axes.

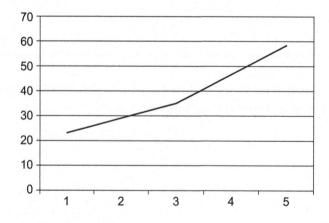

When I draw graphs, the thing I alter (the variable) goes along the bottom axis.

You can download this activity from our website www.routledge.com/ 9781138209053.

Appendix 2.5 Speaking frame – A science experiment

This is an account of an experiment to see

....

....

The equipment needed was

....

....

The method was as follows

....

....

Explain the method using time connectives, e.g.

First ....

Then ....

Next ....

Eventually ....

Meanwhile ....

Use impersonal language and the passive voice, e.g. ....

.... **were placed**

.... **were observed**

.... **was noted**

It was expected that ....

Our findings were that ....

This suggests that ....

(Used with permission from Palmer, S. (2004) *Speaking Frames: Year 6*. London: David Fulton Publishers.)

This is an account of an experiment to see
whether evaporation of water is affected by the temperature.

The equipment required was
three squares of thick card (all the same size), three plastic trays, a stopwatch, a digital thermometer and a bucket of water.

The method was as follows
First, the squares of card were all dipped in the bucket for 10 seconds to ensure they absorbed the same amount of water. They were then placed in the plastic trays and kept at different temperatures: one in the bottom of a fridge, one in a cool outdoor shed and the third in a warm room. The temperature of each location was checked with the digital thermometer. Then the cards were checked at 10-minute intervals to see if they were dry.

It was expected that
the card in the warm position would dry first.

Our findings were that
the card kept in the warm classroom (22°C) dried after 40 minutes; the card in the cool shed (11°C) took 3 hours 50 minutes to dry; the card in the refrigerator (2°C) was still wet after 6 hours.

This suggests that temperature affects the speed at which water evaporates – the warmer it is, the faster evaporation occurs.

Appendix 2.6   Number line and temperature change

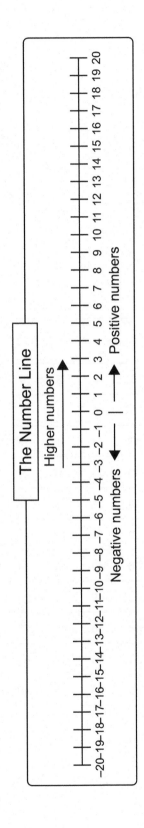

The Number Line

Higher numbers

−20 −19 −18 −17 −16 −15 −14 −13 −12 −11 −10 −9 −8 −7 −6 −5 −4 −3 −2 −1 0 1 2 3 4 5 6 7 8 9 10 11 12 13 14 15 16 17 18 19 20

Negative numbers ◄———— | ————► Positive numbers

The temperature in the freezer was −15°C, but it rose to 7°C when there was a power cut. What was the rise in temperature? Mark the numbers and count between them.

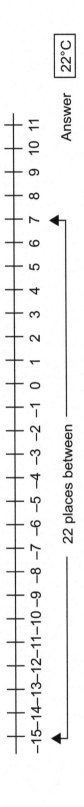

−15 −14 −13 −12 −11 −10 −9 −8 −7 −6 −5 −4 −3 −2 −1 0 1 2 3 4 5 6 7 8 9 10 11

◄———— 22 places between ————►

Answer   22°C

Appendix 2.7   Types of numbers

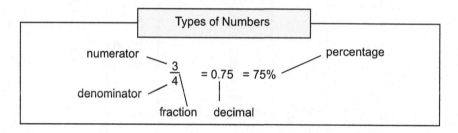

Multiplication – Times Tables

x	1	2	3	4	5	6	7	8	9	10
1	1	2	3	4	5	6	7	8	9	10
2	2	4	6	8	10	12	14	16	18	20
3	3	6	9	12	15	18	21	24	27	30
4	4	8	12	16	20	24	28	32	36	40
5	5	10	15	20	25	30	35	40	45	50
6	6	12	18	24	30	36	42	48	54	60
7	7	14	21	28	35	42	49	56	63	70
8	8	16	24	32	40	48	56	64	72	80
9	9	18	27	36	45	54	63	72	81	90
10	10	20	30	40	50	60	70	80	90	100

Appendix 2.8   Measuring

Length, height, distance

millimetre (mm)

centimetre (cm)

metre (m)

kilometre (km)

1 cm = 10 mm

1 m = 100 cm

1 km = 1,000 m

metre rule

(one metre is a bit more than 3 feet)

Mass

gram (g)

kilogram (kg/kilo)

1 kilo = 1,000 g

(one kilo is a bit more than 2 pounds)

Liquids

millilitre (ml)

litre (l)

1 litre = 1,000 ml

(one litre is a bit less than 2 pints)

Appendix 2.9   Thermometers measure temperature

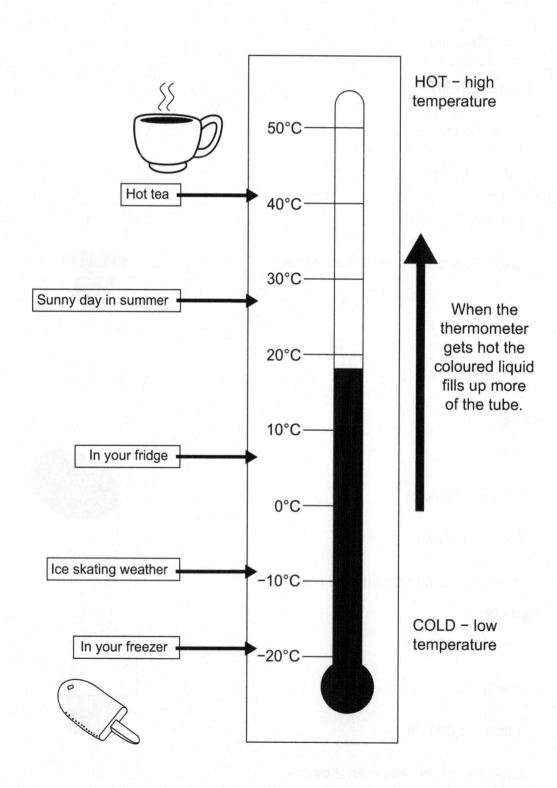

Appendix 2.10   Boiling and freezing

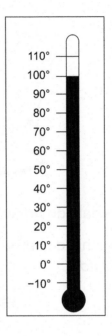

1. *Heating* water to 100°C makes it *boil*.
   When water boils it turns into steam

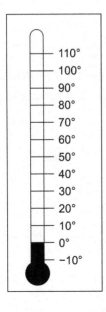

2. *Cooling* water to 0°C or below makes it *freeze*.
   When it's frozen it's completely *solid* – ice

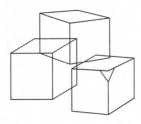

Appendix 2.11 Conductors and insulators – Heat energy

1 Some materials let heat energy pass through them easily.

   a These materials are called *thermal conductors*.

   b *Metals* are good *thermal conductors*.

   c Because heat energy passes through them quickly, metals normally feel *cold*.

Energy

2 Some materials do not let heat energy pass through them.

   a Materials that do not let heat energy pass through them are called *thermal insulators*.

| Cork pot stand | Wooden handle | Oven glove | Thermal vest |

Used to keep food cool

   b Plastic, cork, wood and fabrics are good *thermal insulators*.

   c Thermal insulators are good for keeping heat *out* as well as *in*.

| Cool box | Thermos | Polystyrene cup |

Used to keep hot drinks hot – and cold drinks cold

A *GOOD INSULATOR* = A *POOR CONDUCTOR*

Appendix 2.12 Conductors and insulators – Electricity

1 Conductors let electricity flow through them.

  a Materials that can carry electricity are called *conductors* – they *conduct* electricity.

  b *Metals* such as copper, iron, steel and aluminium are all good conductors.

2 Insulators do not let electricity flow through them.

  a Materials that *cannot* carry electricity are called *insulators* – they don't conduct electricity.

  b Wood, plastic, glass and rubber are all insulators.

| Wood | Plastic | Glass | Rubber |

3 Insulators and conductors both have important uses.

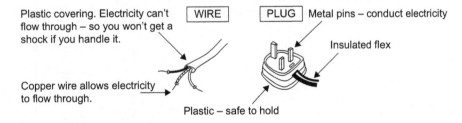

Plastic covering. Electricity can't flow through – so you won't get a shock if you handle it.

WIRE   PLUG Metal pins – conduct electricity

Insulated flex

Copper wire allows electricity to flow through.

Plastic – safe to hold

4 Electricity can be dangerous.

You shouldn't touch *anything* electrical with wet hands – and that includes *switches*. Electricity can be conducted through sweat (salty water) to your body, giving you an electric shock.

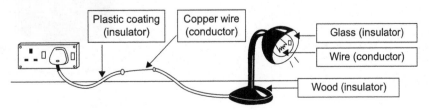

Plastic coating (insulator)   Copper wire (conductor)   Glass (insulator)

Wire (conductor)

Wood (insulator)

Appendix 2.13   Reading scales

exactly 900 ml of liquid

The level is between 40 ml and 50 ml. The lines
between 40 ml and 50 ml divide into 5 equal
portions – so each must be 2 ml. 42, 44, 46, 48 ml.
The liquid is up to the third line from 40 so count
in 2's

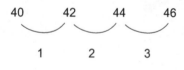

There are 46 ml of liquid

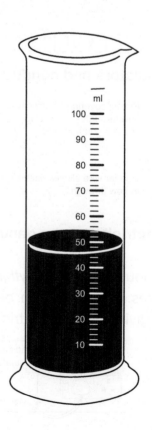

Appendix 2.14   Graphs

The graph shows the temperature of water in a kettle over two minutes.

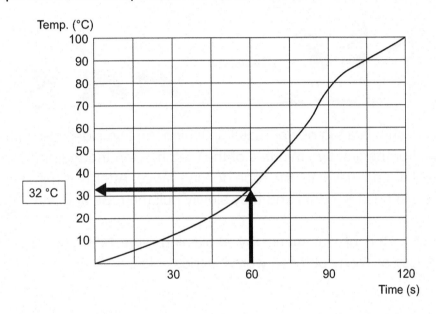

Question: What is the temperature of the water after 60 seconds?

To find out:

1   Find the 60-second mark on the bottom axis and draw a line upwards (vertical) until it meets the graph line.
2   Draw a line across (horizontal) to the side axis.
3   Read the value (temperature on the side axis). The answer is: 32°C

Appendix 3.1   Starter activity – Tug of war

Example activity using a picture as a stimulus

The picture shows a tug of war match in which the two sides are quite evenly matched. For the first two minutes of the match, even though both teams are pulling as hard as they can, the rope doesn't move. After two minutes, one of the sides just has the edge, and they slowly pull the rope and win the match.

Describe this tug of war match by explaining what happens to the forces involved. Use as many of these words as possible:

- Pull
- Balanced
- Unbalanced
- Tension
- Friction
- Accelerate
- Stationary

Appendix 3.2   SMOG test for readability

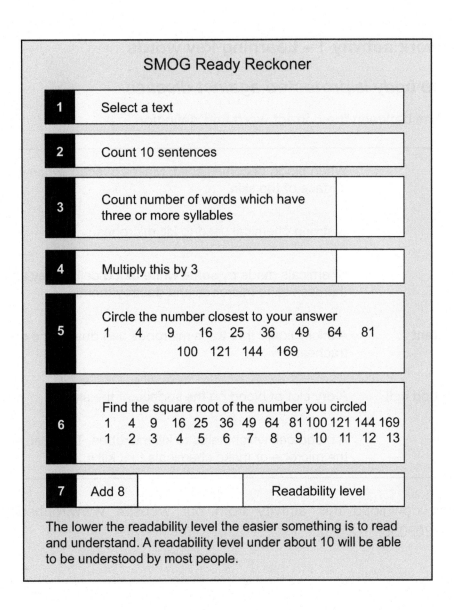

SMOG Ready Reckoner

1	Select a text	
2	Count 10 sentences	
3	Count number of words which have three or more syllables	
4	Multiply this by 3	

5 Circle the number closest to your answer
1   4   9   16   25   36   49   64   81
100   121   144   169

6 Find the square root of the number you circled

1	4	9	16	25	36	49	64	81	100	121	144	169
1	2	3	4	5	6	7	8	9	10	11	12	13

7	Add 8		Readability level

The lower the readability level the easier something is to read and understand. A readability level under about 10 will be able to be understood by most people.

Appendix 3.3   Homework activity

Homework activity 1 – Learning key words

How the body is protected against disease

Draw a line between the correct word and definition.

Scab

When blood becomes solid. Makes a 'scab' when it is on the surface of the skin.

Mucus

A strong chemical used to kill microbes.

Clot

Chemicals made by some white blood cells. They attach themselves to microbes and destroy them.

Disinfectant

A sticky liquid that traps microbes and dust in the nose and trachea.

White blood cell

A dry clot of blood on the surface of the skin.

Antibody

A blood cell which helps to kill microbes. They can surround the microbe or make chemicals that kill it.

You can download this activity from our website www.routledge.com/ 9781138209053.

Homework activity 2 – Research

Letter from an alien

Imagine you are an alien from one of the planets and you are writing to your friend on Earth. Include all the planets you have travelled to, saying what they are like.

Dear ....,

I am your friend, ..., the alien. Your planet Earth is very pleasant because

....

....

I first visited Mercury, but I did not like it because it was ....

....

....

Next I went to Venus, which was pretty because ....

....

....

Then I went to Mars. I wouldn't like to live there because ....

....

....

My spaceship then took me to Jupiter, which has ....

....

....

Even though I was missing home, I continued with my journey and went to Saturn. This planet has ....

....

....

The next planet I flew to was Uranus. This was ....

miles from the Sun.

Neptune has a few interesting features like ....

....

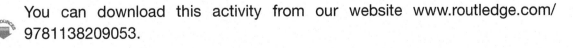

Homework activity 3 – Writing up an experiment

Testing for microbes

The apparatus I used was:

An a _ _ _ p _ _ _ _

A wire loop

Sticky t _ _ _

A b _ _ _ _ b _ _ _ _ _

My method was:

I put the wire loop into the f _ _ _ _ until it was hot.

(I did this so that ....

....)

I dipped the wire loop into the bottle of culture.

I made lines gently on the a _ _ _ p _ _ _ _ with the wire loop.

I put the top on the a _ _ _ p _ _ _ _ and sealed it with sticky t _ _ _.

I then put it in an oven at _ _ °C and left it for two days.

(I did this so that ....

....

....)

You can download this activity from our website www.routledge.com/
9781138209053.

Appendix 3.4   The five-star lesson plan

- Clear learning objectives set for the lesson and shared with the pupils (setting attainable but high expectations)
- The lesson content planned to suit the needs of the pupils, with consideration given to overcoming any barriers to learning; the lesson could contain:

  - Introduction (Not too long. Use modelling/demonstration/video as appropriate.)
  - Main learning activity (Mini plenaries to check understanding and progress and praise good work. Revisit explanations as required and address any misconceptions.)
  - Plenary (Were the learning objectives achieved? Who needs follow-up to ensure completion/better understanding?)

- Any TA support targeted, with clear objectives
- Clearly defined method of monitoring progress
- Evaluation of the lesson for future use (involving TA)

Appendix 5.1   TA strengths and areas for development in science

Name ....

Consider your work within the science faculty

In the following self-assessment procedure, 5 is most effective and 1 is least effective.

1   How do you rate your awareness of the faculty's policies and procedures?

   1   2   3   4   5

2   Underline the areas of science you feel most confident with

biology/chemistry/physics/all

3 What do you consider to be your areas of strength?					
Working with individual pupils	1	2	3	4	5
Working with groups of pupils	1	2	3	4	5
Working within a whole-class setting	1	2	3	4	5
Collaborating with teaching staff	1	2	3	4	5
Working with pupils with particular special educational need (specify type of need)	1	2	3	4	5
Explaining concepts	1	2	3	4	5
Supporting pupils with practical work	1	2	3	4	5
Making differentiated worksheets	1	2	3	4	5
Supporting pupils with literacy	1	2	3	4	5
Supporting pupils with numeracy	1	2	3	4	5
Other					

4   Do you have any particular training needs within science?

....

....

....

....

Please add additional comments you feel are important.

....

....

....

....

Appendix 5.2   Training for teaching assistants working in the science faculty

You need to know the school/science faculty policies on:

- Safety
- Behaviour
- Homework
- Assessment and monitoring

You will need to know how to:

- Light a Bunsen burner
- Heat a test tube in a Bunsen flame
- Heat a beaker of water
- Use a measuring cylinder
- Use a balance
- Use a thermometer
- Use a retort stand
- Use a stop clock
- Filter a mixture
- Evaporate a liquid
- Set up a simple electrical circuit
- Use an ammeter, voltmeter and variable resistor
- Take a pulse
- Find the pH of a substance

Other useful skills include:

- How to draw a graph or bar chart from data collected
- How to use a datalogger
- How to draw a graph using a computer
- Recording results from an experiment

Appendix 5.3 Medium-term planning – Termly

Term Autumn/Spring/Summer .... **Year group** ....

Date	Unit	Key words	Practicals	Adaptations for SEN pupil	Assessments

Appendix 5.4 Short-term planning – Weekly

Teaching group ....

Date	Lesson	Key words	Worksheet needed	Equipment needed	Use of support
	1				
Adaptations needed					
	2				
Adaptations needed					
	3				
Adaptations needed					
	4				
Adaptations needed					

Appendix 5.5 TA planning sheet for science lessons

Science group .... Unit ....

Pupil(s) needing support ....

Date	Lesson	Objectives	Key words	Adaptations/differentiation required
	1			
	2			
	3			
	4			
	5			
	6			
	7			
	8			
	9			
	10			

Additional notes:

Further reading and references

Bloom, B. S. (1976) *Taxonomy of Educational Objectives*, vol. 1. London: Longman.

Booth, T. and Ainscow, M. (2000) *Index for Inclusion*. Bristol: CSIE.

CLEAPSS. (2016) Consortium of Local Education Authorities for the Provision of Science Services. www.cleapss.org.uk

DfE. (2015) *SEND Code of Practice*. London: DfE Publications.

DfE. (2015) *National Curriculum in England: Science Programmes of Study*. London: DfE Publications.

DfEE. (2000) *Working with Teaching Assistants*. London: DfEE Publications.

DfEE. (2001a) *Schools Achieving Success*. Norwich: HMSO.

DfEE. (2001b) *Schools Building on Success*. Norwich: HMSO.

DfES. (2004) *Removing Barriers to Achievement: The Government's Strategy for SEN*. London: DfES.

Kyriacou, C. (1997) *Effective Teaching in Schools: Theory and Practice*. Cheltenham: Stanley Thomas Ltd.

Kyriacou, C. (2001) *Essential Teaching Skills*. Cheltenham: Stanley Thomas Ltd.

Levesley, M., Baggley, S., Clark, J. and Gray, S. (2002) *Exploring Science*. Essex: Longman.

LGNTO. (2001) *Teaching/Classroom Assistants National Occupational Standards*. London: Local Government National Training Organisation.

Lovey, J. (1995) *Supporting Special Educational Needs in Secondary School Classrooms*. London: David Fulton Publishers in association with the Roehampton Institute.

Marvin, C. and Stokoe, C. (2003) *Access to Science: Curriculum Planning and Practical Activities for Pupils with Learning Difficulties*. London: David Fulton Publishers.

McNamara, S. and Moreton, G. (1997) *Understanding Differentiation*. London: David Fulton Publishers.

Millar, R. and Abrahams, I. (2009) 'Practical work: making it more effective'. *School Science Review*, 91(334), 59–64.

Moore, J. (2002) 'The role of observation in teacher appraisal', in Tilstone, C. (ed.) *Observing Teaching and Learning*, 104–121. London: David Fulton Publishers.

Nasen. (2014) *Effective Adult Support* Staffordshire: Nasen.

Ofsted. (2003) *Special Educational Needs in the Mainstream*. London: Ofsted.

Rogers, B. (1997) *Cracking the Hard Class*. Sydney: Scholastic.

Russell, A., Webster, R. and Blatchford, P. (2013) *Maximising the Impact of Teaching Assistants*. London: Routledge.

Sang, D. and Wood-Robinson, V. (2002) *Teaching Secondary Scientific Enquiry*. London: ASE and John Murray.

Sotto, E. (1997) *When Teaching Becomes Learning: A Theory and Practice of Teaching*. London: Cassell.

Stakes, R. and Hornby, G. (2000) *Meeting Special Needs in Mainstream Schools*, 2nd edn. London: David Fulton Publishers.

Warnock, M. (chair) (1978) *Special Educational Needs: Report of the Committee of Enquiry into the Education of Handicapped Children and Young People (The Warnock Report)*. London: HMSO.

Index

Note: Italicized page numbers indicate a figure on the corresponding page. Page numbers in bold indicate a table on the corresponding page.